Sex

AND

Power

SUSAN ESTRICH

RIVERHEAD BOOKS, NEW YORK

Riverhead Books
Published by The Berkley Publishing Group
A division of Penguin Putnam Inc.
375 Hudson Street
New York, New York 10014

First Riverhead hardcover edition: October 2000
First Riverhead trade paperback edition: September 2001
Riverhead trade paperback ISBN: 1-57322-893-1

Visit our website at www.penguinputnam.com

The Library of Congress has catalogued the Riverhead hardcover edition as follows:

Estrich, Susan.
Sex and power / Susan Estrich.
p.   cm.
ISBN 1-57322-124-4
1. Feminism—United States.   2. Sex role—United States.
3. Discrimination against women—United States.   4. Power
(Social sciences)—United States.   I. Title: Sex and power.   II. Title.

HQ1426 .E77   2000   00-042517
305.42'0973—dc21

Printed in the United States of America

10   9   8   7   6   5   4   3   2   1

For Izzy and James

Contents

Acknowledgments

I have been blessed with the most wonderful group of women friends that anyone could have. They are my sisters. I thank them for their friendship, support, and love, and for teaching me that strong women have the power to do anything.

My special thanks to Amanda Urban and Julie Grau; to my students and assistants at Harvard Law School and USC Law School; to Dean Scott Bice of USC Law School, for his support; to Philip Daay, for all his help; to Lynne Wasserman, Pam Fleischaker, Barbara Howar, Kathleen Sullivan, Frances Barnard, Katherine Reback, Nadine Schiff, and Marty Kaplan, for reading various versions of this text and for encouraging me to keep going; to Izzy Kaplan, for caring about women's rights; to James Kaplan, for love; to Annie Gilbar, for the final word and for being there when I needed her; to Judy Jarvis, for her courage in seizing life in the face of death and for sharing her joy in it with me; to Rose Shumow, for inspiration; to my mother, Helen Estrich Kaplan, for dreaming big dreams for me; and especially to my sister Ruth Estrich, who has become my friend as well as my sister. I love you all.

Sex **AND** *Power*

Introduction

"It looked like it was run by twelve union guys who were afraid of the NRA," President Clinton said shortly before he left office. We were talking about the Gore campaign.

If only women had voted, Gore would have won handily. The gender gap that first emerged in the early 1980s was once again a significant factor in explaining the results: women voted for Gore by a 54–43 margin, while men favored Bush 53–42, almost the mirror image.

But the president was also right, and a closer look at the numbers underscore how Gore might have won. While non-white women voted overwhelmingly for Gore, Bush carried white females by a margin of 49–48 percent. Working women favored Gore by a 58–39 margin, but nonworking women gave their votes to Bush by a margin of 52–44. Among unmarried women, Gore carried the day by a 63–32 percent margin, but among married women, there was no gender gap at all.

Even a casual observer of the presidential debates couldn't help but conclude—as I did in frustration, listening to Gore duck a gun-control question that he might have hit out of the park—that he was aiming at the hunters and not the mothers. Meanwhile, candidate Bush had more women, and particularly mothers, working for him than Al Gore ever did. Indeed, it was painful to watch the Gore campaign in the post-election period, no longer even making a pretense of diversity; among the dozens of lawyers and spokesmen for the vice president, not a single woman was seen or heard until Kathleen Sullivan, dean of Stanford Law School, took a red-eye to sit next to Larry Tribe when he argued on Gore's behalf before the Supreme Court.

How does this happen in the year 2000? Sad to say, very easily. Politics is no different from the top ranks of corporate America, where, according to the most recent numbers compiled by Catalyst, the research group that has been tracking women's success in business, women represent just 4.1 percent of the top earners in the Fortune 500—93 out of 2,255, up a glacial .8 percent since last year, up less than 3 percent in the last five years. The pipeline remains overwhelmingly male: of all line officers—those positions with profit and loss responsibility that are viewed as the stepping stone to top jobs—92.7 percent are held by men. As Catalyst concluded, "Women's representation among corporate officers has not changed dramatically in the past five years."

For women of color, the numbers are even worse. Women of color accounted for 1.3 percent of corporate officers in the 400 companies for which Catalyst was able to obtain data, a number unchanged since last year. In these companies, 90 percent of the female officers are white. Exactly six women of color are top earners.

In nothing less than a revolution, Democrats assumed control of the U.S. Senate last spring. But while very few of the Democrats would have been there were it not for the disproportionate share of women's votes they had received, none of the new committee chairs were women. Sixteen Democrats replaced sixteen Republicans as chairmen of the standing committees. Democrats were quick to point out that there were women chairing significant subcommittees, and that it was the system that excluded women, not them. It never seemed to occur to them that if the system doesn't allow Dianne Feinstein, the senior senator from California, to chair a committee, then perhaps there is something wrong with the system.

In the fall of 2001, Harvard Law School, in a historic move, will divide the incoming class into seven sections, each with its own faculty leader. An administrator, in the course of arguing that things are much better for women these days at Harvard, acknowledges that six of the seven "leaders," as well as the two deans, are men—eight out of a total of nine. Better? I'm sure things are better in some ways. But the message being sent to students is a very different one than it would be if Kathleen Sullivan and I were still there teaching first years, as we did before we left; if three out of seven were women, and strong ones at that. If that would be a better message, why doesn't Harvard create a system that promotes it? There are all kinds of good reasons why the women currently at Harvard didn't want to lead sections, I am told. There are all kinds of reasons why Kathleen and I left. But if this result were generally considered unacceptable, they'd find a way to convince these women otherwise, or they'd hire more women. An early retirement is a powerful inducement, if you think you have a problem, if you recognize it as that.

Two new studies of the legal profession point to the troubling conclusion that women may actually be moving backward at the top. This year, more women than men will graduate from law school. Women dominate the bottom of the profession, but the number of women who serve as partners in major law firms in fact decreased last year. While most firms claim to offer part-time opportunities, a miniscule 3 percent of all lawyers take advantage of them, suggesting that part-time remains a dead end and not a detour. The ABA study documents pay gaps at every level based on gender. The Catalyst study found that women plan to leave sooner than men do, which is a self-fulfilling prophecy for life in the second tier. And women of color plan to leave even sooner than white women.

But what is most troubling of all is how easy it has become, for men and women, simply to ignore the persistence of dramatic inequality, to pretend that discrimination doesn't exist, that the absence of women at the top is simply a pipeline problem that will solve itself, or the consequences of women's decisions to be mothers. Three-quarters of the women and 97 percent of the men in the ABA study think that discrimination is no longer a major obstacle for women in the legal profession. Being unconscious of discrimination that is practiced unconsciously confirms it, not eradicates it. When we see a woman who has children leaving the office early, we tend to assume that she has a "kids" event. We take it as proof that she's not as ambitious, not as determined to get to the top. When we see a man leaving early, we assume he's headed to the airport or to a meeting or that there must be some kind of extraordinary emergency. Studies have found that when a woman has a particularly good year, it tends to be largely chalked up by all, including her, to luck; with a man, it's proof of rainmaking ability. And we do all of this unconsciously, by not thinking about gender at all.

I was invited last spring to speak at an elite gathering of "innovators and navigators" jointly sponsored by *Talk* magazine and Paine Webber. It was thick with CEOs, from Disney to General Electric to Starwood Hotels. Of the 200-plus in attendance, all but two of us were white: there were two African-American women, no African-American men, no Hispanics, and no Asians. The women in attendance included many celebrities, almost none of whom had speaking parts during the two days of discussions. Most of the panels, like the opening one on business and the media, included no women at all. Those in attendance who were not called upon to speak included high-tech entrepreneur and industry analyst Esther Dyson; former Texas governor and Democratic keynoter Ann Richards; Barbra Streisand; Donna Karan; Linda Wachner, the CEO of Warnaco; commentators Arianna Huffington and Monica Crowley; Judge Leslie Crocker Snyder; prosecutor Jeanine Piro; HarperCollins president and CEO Jane Friedman; and businesswoman Georgette Mosbacher, among others.

At the first session, I raised the issue of how the media deals with issues of race and gender in business as nicely as I could—I told a story (of the Time-AOL merger and the failure of any news organization to point out that all twenty-four of the operating heads were men) and a joke (from where I sit, I said, you all look alike to me). The subject was dismissed handily: "I'll take that one," *60 Minutes* executive producer Don Hewitt said. "It's easy, I have Lesley Stahl on the air." He did not mention Meredithe Viera, the first woman to join the *60 Minutes* on-air team, who was reportedly fired because she occasionally brought her young children to work, and needed more flexibility than the men she worked with. That was it. Well, I suppose, Don Hewitt was at least willing to address the issue. Later, one of the men on the panel, a very nice young Internet gazillionaire, returned to my question, saying that he wanted me to know he never thought about gender. *That's the problem.*

Perhaps the most disturbing fact was that the conference was organized by women. Tina Brown, the editor of *Talk*, had brought in a team of young women to convene the panelists. Had it ever occurred to any of them that this was a prime opportunity to showcase women and minorities, to give them access to the old boys' network, and the opportunity to shine? I talked to these women afterward. It had not. No one had ever thought of it.

"Why didn't you tell me?" they always ask, years later. My women students, in both my undergraduate and law classes, go out in the world and find that discrimination persists, that the "choices" are illusory, that the mommy track is a dead end with no route back. And many of them are shocked. Of course I told them—and tell them still—but when they're twenty-two or twenty-five, and they haven't met this type of discrimination yet, they simply don't believe me. They don't want to believe such things. Who can blame them?

Even the most successful women I know want to believe that things have changed more than they have. They, too, buy into the fiction that not thinking about gender is the route to equality. Consider what happened to my friend Patt Morrison, just last spring. Patt is a gifted journalist, and, as of this writing, the only female columnist at the *Los Angeles Times*. She came to interview me last year for a profile in *Good Housekeeping*, shortly after her paper had been sold and new men had come from Chicago to run it. She got what I was writing about; she just thought it didn't apply to her. At that time, her column appeared on the front page of the "Metro" section, below the fold, while the choicier real estate on page A3 was occupied by, in my opinion, a rather mediocre male columnist. "What are you doing to protect and promote yourself?" I asked her; her newspaper had a new owner who was bringing new editors and publishers to town. She was doing nothing, except writing a terrific column, hosting a local public affairs show on public television, offering her time to community groups and schools, and the like. She was not running a campaign; she didn't think she needed to. Six months later, the men in charge of the paper announced a restructuring that not only denied her the prized position in the front section; they took her off the front page of the second section, moving her inside, near the weather, which, by the way, in Los Angeles is the same every day.

"Perhaps my judgment is skewed by my maleness," the new editor, John Carroll, wrote to me, in response to my letter of complaint, explaining that he had decided to run the two "best columns we have" (including one that's brand-new,

by a man who hasn't lived here in fifteen years) in the front
section, along with all the ads for Clinique and Estée Lauder
and the white sales that so many men frequent. In the first
week, I forwarded his letter to a hundred or so of my closest
women friends via e-mail, gave out his name and address
twice on C-Span (at the *Los Angeles Times*'s own book fair, at
the session titled by them "What Happened to the Women's
Movement"), and began contacting board members at the
parent company and advertisers who sell their wares to
women in the paper. The answer to what happened to the
women's movement is that too many of us thought we didn't
need it anymore, and we were wrong.

When I was a law student, in the bad old days when firms
made no bones about the fact that there might be one slot for
a woman (not our fault, they would say; our clients just aren't
comfortable with women), I would tell every law firm I inter-
viewed with that I wanted to meet the female partners. Of
course, most of them didn't have any, which my friends and I
on the Women's Law Association's Placement Task Force
knew perfectly well at the time. After all, we were the ones
who'd convinced the Harvard Law School career placement
office to require the firms that used its services to fill out
forms detailing the number of women and minorities who

were associates and partners. "Really," I would say, "no women partners. How unfortunate, I guess you're off my list then."

"Who came up with this stupid form," one partner asked me in an interview one day, assuming that because I didn't need the task force to get a job, I wasn't a part of it. "I did," I said. I laughed all day. You should have seen his face.

Ask to meet the part-time partners, I advise my students, men and women, every year. True, if you're the only one who asks, as I sometimes was, you need very good grades to outweigh your reputation as a troublemaker. But the more people who are willing to ask, the less it becomes an issue of individual troublemakers, and the more it emerges as—dare we say it—an important aspect of firm marketing. At a time when more and more of my female students have given up on making partner before they even begin, there's just no reason to go gently into the night. Ask to meet the top female earners in corporate America (80 percent of the Fortune 500 companies don't have any, and the Fortune 1000 is even worse). Ask how many they have. Ask about maternity leave and paternity leave, and formal mentoring programs; ask whether they've taken affirmative steps to assure that women won't lose out if they don't play golf. Let them know that there are people out there, men and women, who are judging them, who are paying attention to gender, because they aren't.

Raise your hands, I tell young women all the time. Be ambitious. Don't take no for an answer. The world would be a better place if more women were running it, and so long as that is true, then ambition in women should be celebrated as a gift to all of us. Have I bought into their definition of power? Absolutely. I would love to see more women making the decisions that affect the lives of thousands of people and, literally, the policies of nations. More of those decisions in women's hands? Sure. Conventional? Definitely not—and that's the point.

I'm not telling anyone to abandon their children, and I'm not selling motherhood short. I have been blessed with two children, and it is precisely because I consider children and family a blessing, and because I know that there is more to life than money, that I think it so wrong that we don't do more to accommodate the public and the private, work and family.

Those of us who have made it, or gotten close, have a twofold obligation: to help our peers get the last inch, or foot, and to help young women by making it easier for them than it has been for us. What has been missing from the women's movement is women helping women. There's some of it, but not enough. We used to get together for lunch, form our groups, fight against enemies we could see and name. Then we got almost successful enough, and way too busy, and battered in various directions. But we also got more amazing lives than many of us dared dream about and we've got power, if we use it. Don't feel sorry for us. Young women may not want our lives, but we didn't want our mothers' lives, and we haven't gotten them. Even on our worst days, we mostly love our work. We have been blessed, but it is also a responsibility.

I was scared taking on Al Gore on the diversity issue, but I won't be nearly as scared next time around. I've done it once; I survived. I didn't make enough of a difference—the women they brought in never really made it to the inside, or so the men always told me—but it helped. That is incredibly satisfying. It is easy to forget how good it feels to be engaged, to make a difference. My voice shook a little at the *Talk* conference when I stood up to be the skunk at the garden party, to be the one who actually points out what most people would prefer not to notice, but I never doubted for a moment that I would do it. It's what I do. I try to do it as gently and respectfully as I can, but I do it. I collect business cards, and name names. If the editor of the *Los Angeles Times* doesn't like me, I can live with it, if he gets enough e-mail as a result.

I played myself in a Turner television movie last summer, or at least a version of myself. Tom Selleck was running for president, Laura Linney was his campaign manager, and I played the feminist complaining that there weren't enough women in the campaign. In the script, I attack Laura Linney, the brash campaign manager (my old role), for not having women working for her and not being enough of a feminist. It's based, I was told by the producers, on an incident involving Bella Abzug back in the 70s. It is not, I told them, how I would handle such a situation now. Now, I would come up to the woman and congratulate her on her accomplishment. I would tell her I hope things continue to go her way and that one way of ensuring that would be to hire other women and build a team loyal to her, in case the boys should turn on her, as tends to happen in politics, especially if you're the only woman in the room. I'd give her my card and tell her to call if she needed me, and I'd be there to help. And then, twenty pages later in the script, when she's unfairly fired, maybe she'd dig my card out, remember my offer of help, and give me a call. That's the way, given the opportunity, I'd rewrite such scenes—in the movies and in real life.

—Susan Estrich

Los Angeles

June 2001

ONE

In the Middle of
a Revolution

At the dawn of the twenty-first century, Madeleine Korbel Albright, the first woman to serve as secretary of state, the most popular cabinet member at home, a woman both respected and feared by world leaders for her toughness, may well be the most powerful woman in the world. She deserves her power, and she earned it, but that's not exactly how she got it.

I have known Madeleine for twenty years, having been excluded from, and having pushed our way into, many of the same meetings in various campaigns. In the eighties, when visiting potentates sat down with the Democratic foreign policy priesthood, Madeleine figured out that the way to avoid being left out was to invite everyone to her house and cook the dinners, which she did for many years. That way, she got the best seat at the table and began and ended the conversations.

In 1988, Madeleine was in charge of foreign policy as we helped Democratic nominee Michael Dukakis prepare for his first presidential debate. Then Arkansas governor Bill Clinton was in Boston for the day to help. I know it was the first time he saw Madeleine in action; I think it was the first time they'd met. Most members of the priesthood make you feel like an idiot even if you know perfectly well what you're talking about; Madeleine can make you feel smart even if you don't know what you're talking about. The result is that you'll listen better.

It was clear, from that day, how impressed Clinton was with Madeleine and how much he liked her. We all went out for dinner and drinks, and the three of us lasted the longest. But four years later, when Clinton was the nominee, Madeleine and I and a few other women dined together every night during the convention, while the priesthood huddled in a suite dividing offices in the next administration. Or so we assumed.

Madeleine was ultimately appointed ambassador to the United Nations, a job that carries with it a nice apartment in New York, five hundred miles from the circle of foreign policy power. She turned the position into more than it had ever been, because she was smart and politically astute, and maybe also because, there being no women in top foreign policy jobs in Washington, she would get invited to meetings that other UN ambassadors might not. She was an obvious candidate to replace Secretary of State Warren Christopher, a clear shot to be on the short list for the job.

I spoke to a number of women in the weeks before the announcement was expected. Should I write a column about what a great secretary of state Madeleine would be? Should I write to the president, start placing calls to people with his ear? Betty Currie worked for Geraldine Ferraro in 1984, as did a number of other Democratic women my age. We knew about the direct line from Betty to the president long before Monica Lewinsky did. Madeleine has many friends in this group, including Betty. Don't do anything, I was told. Madeleine doesn't want us waging a campaign; we don't think it would help her; the president knows her, for goodness' sake. I didn't disagree.

What happened next made Madeleine secretary of state. A high administration official leaked the short list of candidates to the press. Five men were being considered for the post. Madeleine wasn't on the list. In answer to questions concerning her absence, it was reported that she was in the "second tier."

This time, no one asked. Women—elected officials, pundits, pols, staffers, family members, even the public—responded with outrage at the slight to Madeleine, and made clear how much support she had for the job. In Madeleine's case, many of those expressing outrage had never met her, but they still felt this put-down personally, as women.

"It was the 'second tier' business that did it," Madeleine told me, when I saw her shortly after her appointment. She was convinced that she would never have been appointed secretary of state had it not been for that final put-down.

I think that's true.

But here is the more important distinction: What made the difference for Madeleine was not that the boys put her down—how many times had that happened?—but that the girls stood up. Why did it take one more door slamming to make us do that? Why didn't she ask us? Why did we need to be asked? Just like a woman, you might say. Look at the power

4

that we had that we weren't even using. Imagine what the world might look like if we did.

As a girl growing up, I accepted without question inequities that my daughter would find laughable. *Girls can't read the Torah. Only boys study shop. No girls on the math team. How fast do you type? But he has a wife and family to support. Were you really raped? Women don't do very well here. Don't take it personally; the only reason you didn't get the job was because you're a woman.*

Every society, Margaret Mead observed, divides tasks between men and women, and while the divisions vary with the society, the rankings don't. What the men do, whatever it is, is considered more valuable, which makes men more powerful.

For two centuries, women in our society were confined by law to the separate and lesser sphere of home and family, while men made the rules, controlled the money, and enforced the boundaries of the two spheres. Women were presumed to be better parents, but were prohibited by various state laws from becoming lawyers or serving on juries; a woman could be a waitress but not a bartender, unless her husband or father owned the bar. The justification for the lines, in one form or another, was always at its core the same: women have children. Motherhood was destiny, whether or not you were a mother.

There have always been feminisms, as Wendy Kaminer puts it, but almost all of them start by looking at the world through the lens of gender, and seeing how it matters. A critical perspective challenges the existing order by exposing its political core. What seems inevitable is revealed as socially constructed. Your eyes are opened. *Click,* we called it, the minute you got it. Feminism changed the way I looked at the world. It was as if someone had handed me a new set of questions that I'd never thought of, questions that made clear that it wasn't just me, that I wasn't crazy, that I had a right to better treatment. *Click* meant they wouldn't treat a man this way. It was not the "divine law of the Creator," as one justice put it in denying a woman the right to practice law, but the man-made order that put men on top.

By the time I walked into an employment agency at twenty-one, and was steered to the secretarial/clerical side—notwithstanding my college degree and supposed management experience—I understood that I was being asked how fast I could type because I was a woman, that men had made that decision, that it wasn't fair, and that someday I could put an end to questions like that. I was proud to call myself a feminist.

What I remember isn't just the sense of seeing, but how it made me feel—angry, but also mobilized; ready to do battle, not only for myself, but for the other girls and women. How dare they? "A typewriter," my friend Suzanne used to say, "what an interesting machine. Tell me, how does it work?" "Like hell they don't," I wanted to say to the Harvard professor who told me on my second day of classes that women didn't do very well at Harvard Law School. I thought it, anyway. And I showed him. My women friends brought cookies and support. They took care of me. A year and a half later, I was the first female president of the *Harvard Law Review.* I also headed the National Organization for Women's first task force on employment agency discrimination. Four years after I was raped, I wrote the opinion for the U.S. Court of Appeals for the District of Columbia overturning their rape corroboration requirement.

Feminism didn't just let me imagine that I could break into the boys' clubs, it gave me a reason to want to; a mission that was larger than myself, along with the armor to wear and the comrades to march with. Who could stop us?

There was a legal revolution going on in America. Civil

rights legislation was being enacted and strengthened. While a constitutional equal rights amendment failed to win ratification, feminist lawyers won almost every major case in the Supreme Court, effectively eliminating gender lines from the law. The "men only" signs went down. We put on our dress-for-success suits, convinced we could beat the boys at their own game if only they'd let us play.

They did. We haven't.

Today, equality on the basis of sex is required by law in virtually every area of American life. There is no profession without a significant number of women coming in; in many, there are even a fair number in the middle. But the higher you go, the fewer you find. Thirty years after the passage of antidiscrimination legislation, twenty years after women first entered business and professional schools in significant number, the top ranks of corporate America remain 98 percent male. Most women continue to work in sex-segregated jobs, earning less than men, even when they are better educated. Police and fire departments have been sued, successfully, but 88 percent of police officers and more than 90 percent of firefighters are still men. A recent study of more than 200 job categories found that in all but three, men made more money than women.

Among the top 2,500 top corporate executives in America, there are a total of sixty-three women. Among the Fortune 500, only three companies are headed by women—exactly one more than twenty years ago. The 200 highest paid CEOs in America are all male. After countless "years of the woman," more than 90 percent of Congress is male. One state is dominated by female leaders; the other forty-nine are dominated by men. Women do not run the world. It is still a big story when a woman accomplishes something noteworthy. You still read about the first woman "this" and the first woman "that." Why?

Discrimination remains, albeit a far more subtle version than what I confronted at the desk of the employment agency years ago. The worst of it, these days, is that you can almost never be sure. Would they treat a man this way, I ask myself all the time, when a trade association misleads me to get me to speak for nothing when they are paying all the men; when the computer people at the firm ignore my constant pleas that my machine doesn't work, and then I discover that everyone else but me has been upgraded months ago? So you pitch a fit to get what you deserve, and they call you difficult. Show me a woman over forty who is successful and isn't considered difficult. Why do we have to be difficult to get paid, to get a working computer, to get ahead?

This is not conscious discrimination. No one declared, "Let's not pay her because she's a woman," or "Let's not give her a new computer because she's a woman." They just assumed I didn't need the money as much as the man, that I didn't crunch as many numbers or need to run sophisticated software. Unconscious discrimination is harder to recognize and more difficult to prove, which makes it a more insidious problem for women.

But this is also about us. We don't want it, or we don't want it enough to pay the price, push up the mountain, do what it takes. Women are promoted to partner or president less often than men in corporate America, but they also drop out in much higher numbers; many of those who could make it don't because they never signed up. We take ourselves out of the running, decide that the prize isn't worth it, or that the "mommy track" is good enough, better than killing ourselves to try to change the rules of the game for the next generation while a babysitter tends our children, if we've got to have them.

"For what?" women ask me every day, and I know what they mean.

For what should you give up your life, learn to play golf, and push your head against the wall every day? Who wants to be one of them anyway? We have come up with all the right explanations for why we don't have power, how our kids are more important, and life more worth living, and other things more essential than getting to the top of the slippery pole and telling everyone else what to do. We surrender without a fight. But we pay a price for it.

Everywhere I go, I meet women in their thirties, forties, and fifties, who are ready to go back to work full-time, or launch new lives and careers. They have all the credentials for what they want except that they are ten or twenty or thirty years older than the men and women they are trying to convince to hire them. And as hard as it is to balance and juggle, that is no longer the obstacle, because many of these women are ready to throw themselves in without balance. Their kids are gone; in many cases, so are their husbands.

But certain tracks have been permanently closed, and there's no getting back in, no second chance at bat. One of my older students did a survey of older female law school graduates, and their answers were exactly what you'd expect. They go to interviews with young men their children's age. Who wants to hire his mother to work for him? How is he going to be able to get someone's mother to pull an all-nighter? There's no flexibility for anything less. That's how it is. "How would you feel about going to Disneyland for a summer associate outing?" one older applicant was asked. She said she'd feel fine, she'd taken her children many times. It was not the right answer. "What was I supposed to do at Magic Mountain?" a former student of mine lamented. "Even my kids are too old for it."

"Dot.coms," you say. Surely those twenty-five-year-olds running Internet companies who work even longer hours than the lawyers and don't dress as well will open their doors wide to suburban women who missed the first part of this revolution. Dream on. This is a world where forty is old, and part-time barely exists. I love the exceptional stories as much as the next person, but I hear many more from women who just assumed there would be more choices, who thought they were doing the right thing by putting their families first. In the meantime, more than 95 percent of all venture capital goes to men.

Our life expectancy keeps getting longer, and yet the only years women can make it are precisely those years when we can have children. Why do this to ourselves, collectively speaking? Why set up a workplace where the only way to succeed is to pull an all-nighter? You may have less energy at fifty, but you have more experience, maturity, stability, and loyalty, which should count for something. How senseless not to take full advantage of that, not to figure out ways that those who don't fit in the round hole can nonetheless contribute. How many overqualified real estate brokers can a neighborhood support? How many degrees are going unused, potential untapped?

When people are not allowed to participate to their full capacity, when their autonomy is trampled and their spirits crushed, we all lose. It is not simply a question of victimhood, but of our collective loss. If it weren't for gender—if it weren't for the fact that it is middle-aged women who are being excluded, which doesn't seem unusual—the loss would be obvious.

And I meet younger women who may be destined to continue on that very path. It is a measure of how far we have come that so many young women today could believe that they don't face discrimination. They don't see a workplace structured for people with no child-care responsibilities as inherently discriminatory. When you point out how few women there are on top, they shrug and say, "Who wants to be there?" In the first five minutes, a female law review president will tell you that she doesn't want to live like a man or like the hard-driving women of my generation. She's not planning to make partner. Two years, and then pregnancy, and then who knows? I have never, ever heard a male law review president talk like that.

And what do I tell them when they send the baby announcements, go part time, tell me in advance that they have no intention of climbing the corporate ladder because they want to have a family? Do I tell them that they may be very, very wrong, may find themselves shut out later, may be demanding too little of others, including their husbands as well as their employers?

I do not. How could I? I say congratulations. I wouldn't trade my family for more power, or a partnership, or a presidential campaign. I joke that now I'm president of the "negligent mothers club," but for me, going on field trips comes before going on television. I got further in my career before having children, which gives me control that most young mothers don't have, but I also paid the price of waiting. The only time I ever regretted running a presidential campaign was when my fertility doctor told me that I might be too old to have a second child. I was lucky, and blessed; my son is seven now, but if I'd known what was ahead of me, would I have waited?

It was not so many years ago that women who did not work outside the home saw themselves as the victims of the nightmare cocktail question: "What do you do?" Deborah Fallows wrote a book nearly two decades ago based on her decision to leave the paid workforce to raise her children, and faced social ostracism for doing so. Today, dropout moms are pictured on magazine covers happily trading in their briefcases, and the saying that "no one on her deathbed ever said she spent too little time at work" trips off tongues.

What sets tongues wagging is women who are "too ambitious." Women who put work ahead of family, women who marry for ambition, or stay married for it; these are women who make other women uncomfortable. In my generation, there's a name for it—Hillary.

One way to look at Mrs. Clinton's aspiration to public office is as a role model for other fifty-somethings who have put their ambitions on hold while supporting their husbands' careers. There is a genuine "my turn" aspect that you'd think women would find appealing. But many of them don't. In the weeks after Mrs. Clinton announced her senate candidacy, the big story was Hillary's "woman problem." Particularly among suburban white women, the initial reaction to the Clinton candidacy was overwhelmingly negative. Some polls among these women had her trailing by thirty points.

"Who does she think she is?" one after another suburban

woman told reporters sent to find out what women don't like about Hillary Clinton. Other comments sounded similar themes: too ambitious, too arrogant. "How does she leave the house," women were asking in the midst of the Monica-mess, "much less run for Senate?" Why does she put us through this? Even the liberal and loyal Ellen Goodman was wringing her hands, reduced to the argument that Hillary wasn't running against Hillary but against Rudy Guiliani, who would be much worse for women.

Hillary Clinton is a woman who wants to be in the center of the debate, on the cover of the magazine, on the floor of the Senate, and is willing to pay a price to get there. She thinks she's someone with something to say. She wants power. She was much more popular when she was standing by her man.

My girlfriends from law school started pulling back five to ten years after we graduated. Biological alarms blaring, they went in-house, of counsel, PTA. All the men I knew who'd gone to firms made partner. A day's mail could easily include a partnership announcement from a man and a baby announcement from a woman. "How many of your female classmates have become law firm partners?" Judge Shirley Abrahamson, the first woman to serve on the Wisconsin Supreme Court, asked me. I was counting the women on one hand, compared to dozens of men, ratios that bore no relation to the composition of my law school class. She was horrified. The balance is impossible, I explained. She didn't disagree. But how are you going to take over if you're all dropping out? You can't change the rules if you're not in the room. You can't finish a revolution without getting in there and fighting. Women had been entering law in increasing numbers for more than a decade. What happened to the army?

I knew what my friends would say. All well and good. But this child has one mother. I have said the same thing many times in the last ten years. We put our families first.

In a man's case, putting his family first means providing for them. Men leave home, stay married, go weeks without seeing their families, and no one criticizes them for being ambitious. They set their sights high. We call them successful. Smart. Doing what it takes to succeed. When women do the same thing, we shake our heads. Too Hillary. A friend who is a successful businesswoman and the mother of four finds herself cross-examined by women she doesn't even know about how she is raising her children. Mothers who climb Mt. Everest are viewed differently than fathers who do, especially by the mothers who don't.

Consider the case of one very ambitious young woman

who I came to know, Gina Occan of Lakewood, California. The conventional wisdom is that younger women are less ambitious than baby-boom feminists. Not Gina. She had a full scholarship at Harvard and had just finished her freshman year with a 3.5 grade point average when she came home for the summer and fell head over heels in love with Tomasso, the son of wealthy Orange County restaurant owners. Most of us have known someone like Tomasso. Handsome and irresponsible, he rode a motorcycle, wore fancy clothes, and swept Gina off her feet. It was a summer romance. He must have been irresistible to a girl who had spent her high school years making straight A's in an all-girl Catholic school, and living in a small apartment with a mother who was determined that her daughter get the sort of education and opportunity that a teenage pregnancy had made impossible for her.

When she discovered she was pregnant, Gina returned home to have the baby, never seriously considering an abortion. She and Tomasso planned to return to Cambridge with their new daughter the next fall, where Tomasso would find work as a waiter while Gina completed her education. But after a series of quarrels, Gina and her baby moved out. Three days later, Tomasso sued for custody.

Tomasso's argument was that the child would be better off

in southern California, where his parents could help take care of the baby, than in Cambridge, where she would be in day care for long days and nights. Tomasso and his parents won the first round, securing a temporary order that blocked Gina from taking the child out of state without permission. Instead of going back to Cambridge in September to begin her sophomore year, Gina went on welfare.

She was on welfare when I met her. To save money on attorneys, she spent her free time in a local law library, researching her rights. Even more important, she began a campaign to win the attention of the local stringer for the *Los Angeles Times,* believing that she needed publicity to reverse the decision of the local court and that the deck was stacked against her in Orange County. After weeks of peppering the stringer with letters, he wrote a short article for the newspaper about the girl who was being blocked from taking up a scholarship to Harvard. I had a talk radio show at the time in Los Angeles. I am a feminist, a former Harvard professor, a scholarship student. This story was irresistible.

Gina came up to Los Angeles a number of times to appear on my show, often bringing Baby Bailey with her. My own daughter would come with me on those days to play with the baby. My young producer, closer in age to Gina than I am, became her friend and confidante. We helped find her a high-profile lawyer who would take the case without a fee, and turn it into a feminist cause célèbre; we called in our contacts with local and national television to build pressure for her position. We vilified the judge at every opportunity. How dare he? How could he? What century was he living in? He reversed himself.

A few weeks after he did, I was having a conversation with a friend of mine, a woman—herself a judge—whom I respect enormously. She was troubled by the case, because she knew the judge—he had actually been a student of hers when she was teaching part-time—and he wasn't a bad guy. We might be vilifying him as a sexist demon of another era who would deprive a hard-working girl of the Harvard education that she had dreamed of, but that wasn't the guy she knew. Could there be more to the case than met the eye?

I had never asked Gina whether any other colleges or universities had offered her a full scholarship. After all, I'd spent most of my adult life at Harvard. But one of the television reporters, in one of the last interviews, did. The answer was yes. The University of Southern California (USC) had offered her a full scholarship. It turned into a very negative story. It made the point that Gina could have been attending classes at

USC instead of doing legal research and going on welfare. If she had taken the USC option, she might never have gotten the judge's decision reversed. But would her child have been better off?

How do you compare a father's desire to see his child on a regular basis with a mother's ambition to go to Harvard? How do you compare a relationship with grandparents who love a baby and want to care for her while her mother is in school, to a Harvard education and care by strangers 3,000 miles away? Was choosing USC over Harvard really too big a sacrifice to ask of an ambitious young woman?

It is a hard question, particularly for me. After ten years as a Harvard professor, after winning tenure and earning the title "Professor of Law," something few women had done, I resigned from Harvard Law School to teach at USC. My feminist colleagues, all four of them, were pretty much appalled. So were most of my male colleagues. I did it because I wanted a family. No one could think of a single man who had ever left Harvard to accommodate his wife. But after four years of commuting between Los Angeles and Boston, I had to make a choice. My daughter was born the next year. Three years later, my son followed. For years, I gave speeches about why my decision not to live by the boys' rules—not to let ambition, as they defined it, define me—was the best decision of my life. So why was I vilifying the judge for imposing the same set of priorities on Gina? Why was I helping her get her way? If Gina was right, had I somehow been wrong?

Women's groups are always a little taken aback when I read them the numbers from the various surveys, or just read down the list of major American corporations with one or no women on their boards in 1999. Everyone smiles in recognition when I tell stories about pitching a fit to get a computer, or trying to learn golf to fit in, or the kids who give it to their working moms. Been there. But somehow, even we are surprised by the numbers, having assumed—blame it on our gender training—that maybe it was just us.

For a while, when I gave speeches, I would carry around pictures of the two sides in the negotiation of the 1998 federal budget agreement. There is one picture of the Democrats, with the president walking away from the camera arm in arm with two men, who are each arm in arm with two more men, who are next to two more men. At the very end, struggling to keep up, is the back of Janet Yellin, the chairman of the council of economic advisers, the least powerful person in the picture, the only woman. On the other side, I have a picture of three dozen Republicans surrounding then Speaker Newt Gingrich, which looks particularly good on an overhead as thousands of eyes scan what might be, by my best guess, a female nose. The rest are male faces. But it's only the federal budget, I tell my audience. Nothing really important. It's only the Fortune 1000 that's 98 percent male at the top.

Is it really this bad?

The answer is no, which is what makes this moment an interesting one. It's not because the numbers are wrong, or because they use sloppy methodology, charges that some conservative women were reduced to making in response to the finding of a pay gap even at the very top, even controlling for everything.

We are not powerless. We are not in the same place we were ten years ago, or twenty years ago. I have lived those years, taught law during those years, banged my head against a few walls myself. And I have watched things change.

The issue all those men in the budget negotiations were discussing at the end was money for education, and the Democrats got more than they thought they would because the Republican negotiators were loathe to be labeled as anti-education, viewed as the "kiss of death" to female voters. There is a women's vote in this country, and it is a pro-child, pro-education, pro-choice vote, statistically speaking. There is hardly a politician of either party who does not understand the power of the "women's vote," of women's ways of looking at things differently than men, and their increasing willingness to express it, and to expect their agenda to be addressed. It may be all men in the room, but women put a good many of them there, and they know it.

We make 83 percent of all consumer purchases. We outlive men, and end up controlling as much as 90 percent of the wealth, depending on which studies you believe. Everywhere we turn, companies are appealing to us, as women, to buy their cars, fly their airlines, stay in their hotels, buy their cereal, take their vitamins, wash with their detergents or shampoos, even invest with their brokers.

The gloom and doom version of feminism has its numbers right, but it's all trees and no forest. American women have enormous power at their fingertips, particularly middle-class American women. They have more skill, more wealth, more political and consumer clout than ever before in history, more power than any group of women in the world. More power, if and when we choose to use it.

That's the punch line. Will we bring ourselves to use our power? Can we bring ourselves to recognize our common interest as women, and wield power on the basis of it? How many times must they say no before we do? Even to Madeleine Albright?

I am giving a speech to my Temple sisterhood at a beautiful brunch. I tell the story of a woman who decided to launch a proxy campaign to join her local all-male bank board, and won; she was a respected lawyer who had finally had it with asking; she got a list of the shareholders, mailed letters explaining her candidacy to all of them, and won. "Anybody in this room know how to do a mailing?" I ask the roomful of women. Get a list? Follow-up phone calls? That's what it takes to put together a sisterhood brunch, of course.

But that's only the beginning. The women in front of me, many of them my age, have plenty of experience in the public world. They could take on any board in the country if they used it. There are women who do public relations, lawyers, advertising execs, former bankers, artists, activists. If they were to decide today that United Airlines had gone long enough without a single woman on its board (as I write, they have none), I'd give it a week. I'd write the column. Maybe we could demand two women. It would be fun, even. So why don't we? Would things be better or worse if we did?

As a television commentator, you're paid to disagree. It's

cheap entertainment; I've always thought it would be much more interesting to see on what points adversaries agree, but I don't run the show. I was busy disagreeing with Jennifer Dunn, a conservative Republican congresswoman, about Hillary Clinton or Monica Lewinsky when we stumbled upon a major agreement. "Would the Congress be a different place if half the representatives were women?" she was asked. She thought it would be, and I agreed. Do you have any doubt?

Imagine what the world would be like if half the nations' leaders were women. Imagine if half the leaders in our own country—governors, senators, city council, everything—were women. Would the schools be better, worse, or just the same? Would there be better support for childcare?

Imagine if half the insurance companies were run by women. Would contraceptives be covered? Would legislation be required so women could see a gynecologist?

Imagine if half the entertainment companies were run by women. Would there be different video games?

Imagine if half the Fortune 500 companies were run by women. Would more doors be open to women returning to the workforce? Would men find it easier to take paternity leave? Would there be more women in the number two and three and four jobs than there are now? Madeleine Albright has more women at the top than any previous secretary of state. Granted not every woman helps those below her, but qualified women still tend to hire other qualified women faster than men do.

Most women in America don't consider themselves feminists, which is continually cited as a measure of the failure of women's rights to capture the imagination of American women. Many young women who are its most prominent beneficiaries run fastest in the opposite direction. But it doesn't really matter what people call themselves. Given how feminism has been practiced by radicals, caricatured by the media, and maligned by its opponents, it's impressive how many women do call themselves feminists, and how "feminism" manages to live on notwithstanding the declaration of its death on a newsmagazine cover at least once every five years.

What matters is how we women view ourselves and our progress. Do we see ourselves as women? Do we see women as equal to men? A 1997 poll by Peter Hart and Associates for NBC News concluded that 65 percent of American women believe that the country has not yet done enough to ensure equality for women. Other surveys back that up. The *New*

York Times Magazine reported in a 1999 issue celebrating women that, at the rate we're going, it will be another 270 years before women achieve parity as top managers in corporations and 500 years before we achieve equality in Congress. Why in the world would we want to go at that rate?

Most professions are not organized to accommodate a woman's biological clock. The periods of most intense work are often just when it's time to have kids. Unconcious assumptions continue to block the paths of women trying to play by the rules, whether or not they are mothers. Important interactions take place around events that most women don't engage in. It is way too difficult to take time off to have a family and then come back and have a chance to fulfill your potential. The problem with the "mommy track" isn't that it represents a detour. A detour would work. The problem is that it's a dead end.

But none of that has to be the way it is. Two decades ago, the professions that are now sending women down dead ends didn't even admit them, and official firm functions in corporate America were routinely held at locations where women were simply excluded. If a woman wanted to attend, she had to enter by a back door and go to a private room. Routine.

The purpose of recognizing discrimination is not to

become a victim, but a revolutionary. When I signed on, the idea was to get women to the top who would then change the rules for everyone. The first wave would pry open the door and then throw it wide open. But the first wave turned into a trickle. The Hillarys and Ginas are the exceptions, not the rule, suspect even by those who stand to benefit from their success, caught by a double standard composed by women as well as men. Even those of us who support them mostly don't want to be them. The rules are not on our side, and we know it. But we have the power to change them.

Very few companies have women on top, but almost every company has three senior women who can command attention if they act together. Almost every company depends on women as consumers. Legislative action may persuade companies that it is indeed possible to be both flexible and profitable; that has been the experience ever since the federal government started requiring larger employers to provide unpaid family leave. As women, we have the power to force any institution in our society to take notice, if we work together. But sometimes, even those of us in the business of power forget what we have. Even Madeleine Albright.

We have struggled for legal equality, and at least by some definitions, we've gotten it. But what we need isn't just equality. It is change. The only way to free the individual woman to become all that she can is for women to act as women, to wield power as women, so that as individuals we can be free. That is what made feminism a revolution. It's just not finished.

TWO

On Being
Extraordinary

I am racing out after giving a speech to a mother-daughter luncheon for the graduating seniors at a local school. I am racing to see my own children; some of the seniors will be racing out, as soon as the next speaker finishes, so they can complete their English papers. On the way out, I run into a mother and daughter, leaving early. Is it the English paper, I ask? "No," the mother explains, "it's me." This senior has a mother in the financial services industry. Always on the look-out for stories and lessons, I ask her how she does it. She laughs bitterly. "I got the job because they thought I was thirty-four and didn't have kids. The truth was that I was forty-four and had four kids. Years have gone by, and they still don't know how old I am, much less about the kids."

Maybe they wouldn't care anymore; I'd bet she's very good at what she does, makes a lot of money for them, and has more power than she realizes, but not as much as men who do what she does. But there is more: The only reason she got the job, at thirty-four with no kids, was because a woman was doing the hiring. She was willing to take the risk on the thirty-four-year-old non-mother, but even she wouldn't have hired a middle-aged woman with four kids.

Why not? Not because she sits down and says, I don't like middle-aged women with kids. Some of her best friends are, no doubt, middle-aged women with kids. The firm doesn't have a policy on not hiring women; my guess is that their policy is quite elaborately just the opposite, administered by a human resources professional who in all likelihood is herself a woman. The men who actually run the firm were educated with women in their business classes; broke into the profession with women working side by side; are probably married to women who have worked outside the home, even if they don't do so now; and have daughters at home for whom they have high hopes and expectations. They are men who would be surprised if you told them they discriminate; it is not their experience of themselves.

Their views mirror those of a new generation of women who have never confronted explicit discrimination. They always read the Torah and take it for granted that there are girls on the math team. They think it is all different for them, and on the surface it is. But look deeper, and attitudes have barely changed.

There are certain assumptions that almost everyone makes about women, particularly about women with children, much less four of them—assumptions about how hard they'll work; how driven to succeed they are; or how willing they will be to take on the impossible challenge at the last minute, to travel at a moment's notice, to put work before everything else. The assumptions applied to mothers slip over; they become assumptions applied to women, if not about children, then still about ambition, need, and toughness. Thinking about women as mothers entails more than the hours they devote to childcare.

The assumption is that a man with children will work harder to support his family, while a woman with children will work less to be with her family. The assumption is that men are ambitious, that work is what matters most, and that women are more concerned with balancing their lives than with getting ahead. Women who have children are assumed to work less; women who don't, to need less. Women with working husbands need less because they have two incomes in the family; women without them need less because they have no one to support. Men are assumed to want more and are given it without asking; women are assumed to want less, and they validate it when they don't ask, don't demand, and don't get what they need and deserve.

To succeed, a woman must prove herself extraordinary, different from other women, better than men; and even those women face additional obstacles because they are women. Most women, who aren't different, who are mothers, are all but excluded from the competition by neutral rules whose application is anything but neutral. Qualifications are defined as they always have been. The burden falls on a woman to figure out how to make the corporate culture comfortable with her, not the other way around. Women remain the other, fighting assumptions that don't apply or apply too much about the ways in which they are different from men.

Ask successful corporate women what the key to their success is, and first and foremost, they cite a record of always exceeding expectations. Because less is expected, more is required.

In studying success stories in corporate America and talking to hundreds of women who have spent time in the trenches, it is absolutely clear that a woman who hopes to penetrate the top ranks must affirmatively prove that the assumptions about working women, and working mothers in particular, do not apply to her. There is no subtlety in the advice.

"There are several key points when a woman's career is jeopardized—when they get married, when they get pregnant, when they take a maternity leave," according to Arlene Johnson, a researcher at the Families and Work Institute. "At those critical points, it's a good idea to make it clear that you're going to return and what your goals are. Often, to compete with males, women have to forgo, or camouflage, their family interest to show their commitment."

The assumptions that motherhood is usually an obstacle to women's success and that women are less ambitious than men are precisely the sort of traditional stereotypes condemned by the Supreme Court in defining sex discrimination. Not every woman becomes a mother and not every woman who becomes a mother limits her hours, travel, and ambition on that account. There are, after all, women like the managing director of a major investment bank who was thirty-five and pregnant with her first child when the firm decided to close its Los Angeles office. She went into labor while her husband, a money manager, was working in Tokyo; complications nearly killed her and her baby. Nonetheless, when the baby was five months old, she moved to Chicago on her own, leaving the baby in Los Angeles with her in-laws, and commuted back on weekends. She did that for a year, until her husband retired and moved with their son to Chicago. There are women like Paula Sneed, a top executive at Kraft, whose husband took care of their teenage daughter full-time while Paula commuted between their home in New Jersey and her office in Illinois, and women like Bonnie Fuller, a magazine editor, whose husband stays home to care for their children.

Irene Rosenfeld, who heads the desserts and snacks division of Kraft, one of America's most women-friendly companies (half of the ten operating divisions were run by women, as of 1996, compared to 5 percent or less nationally) says she works seven days a week, ten to twelve hours a day, and travels 30 percent of the time—figures that seem fairly standard at that level. Her colleague, Mary Kay Haben, who runs the pizza division, schedules both her personal and professional life in detail six months in advance, lives within walking distance of work, and keeps toys in the office for weekends. "Part of being successful is being available and visible all the time," she told a reporter, in explaining her success at Kraft. So powerful are the assumptions to the contrary—that women won't be available, won't work as hard—that women must go to extraordinary lengths to disprove them.

Carol Bartz was diagnosed with breast cancer two days after taking over as chief executive of Autodesk, Inc., in 1992. She opted for a stopgap lumpectomy and continued working for another month before undergoing a radical mastectomy, and then returned to work four weeks after the surgery, rather than the six to eight weeks that doctors recommend. "Having a female illness," she later explained in a published interview, "I thought this could be fodder for anyone inclined to question whether a woman should be doing this job, and I wanted to avoid that at all costs."

The resignation of Brenda Barnes from her position as head of PepsiCo Inc.'s North American beverage business to spend more time with her family provoked an angry response precisely because it operated to reinforce the assumption that women with children will work less, be less ambitious, be more prone to walk away. Ms. Barnes's "unprecedented candor" in explaining what her executive climb had cost her—years of constant travel, living apart from her husband, and missing her three children's birthdays—turned her into a lightning rod, according to writer Sue Shellenbarger, ace chronicler of the work-family juggle, who reported that her voicemail at the *Wall Street Journal* literally crackled with the angry voices of women workers. "This has set the rest of us back a long time," one woman said. "It verifies all the worst stereotypes about women in the workplace." She should have lied, according to a market consultant who had herself been the victim of discrimination. "The workplace isn't the place for frankness. If it were, your boss would be able to say during a review, 'I'm not promoting you because I don't like you.' Women on her level should exert a little creative spin." Men with stay-at-home wives took it as vindication of their efforts, proving "that you can't have it all, be supermom, and superexecutive, too."

Over the years, I have talked to hundreds of the most successful women in America about how they run their lives. What I have learned will surprise no one. If they have children at home, they have help twenty-four hours a day, seven days a week. There is always a babysitter available. Most of them don't have children. If they have husbands, they tend to be extraordinary as well in how few demands they place on their wives and how much responsibility they assume for the household and for the family, not to mention how comfortable they are having a wife who may be more successful than they are and may earn more money.

Consider the case of Carly Fiorina, much in the news in the summer of 1999 after her selection to be the CEO of Hewlett-Packard, the first woman to head a blue-chip corporation. Fiorina has told reporters that gender had nothing to do with her promotion and her success. But to call Fiorina extraordinary doesn't begin to describe the reality. Her husband actually took early retirement to support her career ambitions. He told friends that he realized her career had more potential than his, and if one of them didn't quit, they would simply never see each other. So he did. The father of two grown daughters from a previous marriage, Frank Fiorina may be even more extraordinary than his wife.

What makes Fiorina's story most unusual is that unlike most other extraordinary women, she actually made it to the top. She is undoubtedly right that gender played no role in her career, but that is the exception. According to the studies, even women who make it to the top, or close to it, make less than their male peers. The women who are full professors are less likely to be department heads, and the department heads are less likely to become deans. Associates are less likely to become partners, and partners are less likely to run the firm. Vice presidents are less likely to become presidents and CEOs. Fiorina brings to three the number of women heading Fortune 500 companies. Three is the most there have ever been. Is it because there are only three women in America qualified to head a large corporation? Or is it because qualified women don't get recognized as such?

One common explanation for the wage gap at the top is that women tend to be concentrated in staff jobs (working under a man) rather than holding line responsibilities, and running their own show. But in a study by Catalyst, the New York research and advocacy organization founded by Felice Schwartz in 1962, of top earners, published in the *Wall Street Journal* in November 1998, the top-earning women in line positions still earned less than the men in staff positions. Corporate top earners, like law firm partners, surgeons, engineers, MBAs, and tenured professors, earn less if they are women.

The higher you go in the work world, the more difficult it is to adduce objective proof of why someone isn't being promoted, or what factors entered into their pay package. It may be true, as the Catalyst study of top earners suggests, that putting a woman's name at the top of the resumé automatically reduces the likely salary and bonus package, but we don't have "testers" for top jobs in the same way we do for housing discrimination, where blacks and whites of equal income apply to rent the same apartment to see who is accepted. These are subjective decisions in which no two people are exactly alike, and in which the tendency of the decision maker to prefer someone who looks just like him is unconscious and almost inevitable. I vividly remember sitting in Harvard Law School faculty meetings and hearing one professor after another extol the virtues that he had in common with the would-be hire; Ph.D.'s always thought a Ph.D. essential, while former Supreme Court law clerks would always focus on that particular line in the resume. Objective? Hardly. But how do you prove that it is discriminatory?

Most of the studies finding that women are paid less than men, controlling for all of the obvious factors, do seem to prove that the key factor producing the disparity must be gender. But they do not establish how or why gender operates this way, and in a world in which most decision-makers are utterly unconscious of any bias, and indeed feel just the opposite, the studies' conclusions tend to be immediately questioned, as the Catalyst study was, or attacked because the sample is so small (there aren't many women at the top), or dismissed as mere coincidence rather than as a pattern of discrimination. Given the subjectivity of judgments at this level, how do you prove discrimination? There will always be some other factor that can be invoked, not only by the decision-maker, but by the woman herself. Maybe I just wasn't good enough, we say to ourselves. Maybe it's just me.

In one famous case, Nancy Ezold sued the Philadelphia law firm she had worked at for failing to make her a partner, claiming that equally or less qualified men were admitted to the partnership, while she was denied. She actually won in the district court, managing to convince the judge that it was gender and not performance that had been the critical factor. On appeal, the United States Court of Appeals for the Third Circuit reversed the decision, holding that the law firm had met its burden of coming forward with a nondiscriminatory reason for denying her the partnership promotion—that her legal analysis ability fell below the firm's standard—and that Ezold had failed to prove that the stated reason was merely a pretext for discrimination. The court upheld the partnership's right to make its decisions based on a "subjective consensus among the partners," emphasized a company's "right to make business judgments on employee status, particularly when a decision involves subjective factors deemed essential to certain positions," and cautioned courts against "unwarranted invasion or intrusion" into matters involving professional judgments.

This is what makes the 1999 MIT study so important. This study focused not on the treatment of entry-level women on its faculty, whose biggest concerns tended to relate to balancing family and work, but on how the very few women who made it to the level of tenured, senior professors were treated. These were women who did not expect to be discriminated against and were surprised to discover that they had been.

The impetus for the MIT study grew out of conversations among three senior women in the summer of 1994 about the quality of their professional lives. While each of them had come to realize, individually, that gender had probably caused their careers to differ from those of their male colleagues, they had never discussed the issues with one another, and were uncertain about whether their perceptions were in fact accurate or their experiences unique. Once they began the discussion, they realized that their experiences in fact formed a pattern, and the idea of a full-scale study was born.

What the committee found, in the words of Professor Lotte Bailyn, the chair of the MIT faculty, "is that gender discrimination in the 1990s is subtle but pervasive, and stems largely from unconscious ways of thinking that have been socialized into all of us, men and women alike." The committee documented difference in overall salaries, in salaries from grants, in access to space, resources, and inclusion in positions of power and administrative responsibility. The result of these differences were that women had less, felt marginalized, and were excluded from professional opportunities. The problems appeared to increase progressively as women aged and as they approached the same age as their administrators. As of 1994, the percent of women on the MIT faculty had not changed significantly for at least two decades. Once the committee's recommendations began to be implemented, those numbers increased for the first time in twenty years.

Until the study was done, MIT's defense was that its percentage of female faculty members was no lower than other universities, or corporations for that matter. Indeed, there seems to be something almost magical about the figure of 8 percent: it appears over and over again in tenured faculties, firm partnerships, and management jobs. Because they did not experience themselves as consciously discriminating, and because their percentages were in line with those of other comparable universities, the men at MIT were able to convince themselves that they didn't have a problem, or at least not a significant one.

The lesson for the men was critical. Dr. Charles Vest, the president of MIT, acknowledged: "I have always believed that contemporary gender discrimination within universities is part reality and part perception. True, but I now understand that reality is by far the greater part of the balance." And he admitted to sitting bolt upright when a senior woman, who had felt unfairly treated for some time, said, "I also felt very positive when I was young." Professor Robert J. Birgenau, dean of the MIT School of Science, made clear that he understood that even though the discrimination against women was "usually totally unconscious and unknowing," that "the effects were and are real." And perhaps most important, he affirmed that he understood the stakes: having a faculty that "remains overwhelmingly white and male . . . means that we are not taking advantage of the tremendous talents of the absolute majority of the population in filling our faculty ranks. This is to the detriment of the students, the faculty, and MIT as a whole. Correcting this extreme imbalance is one of the major challenges that MIT faces as we enter the next millennium."

But the lesson for the extraordinary women who thought that they had made it to the top, or at least as far as they deserved, was even more important. Even extraordinary women—*especially* extraordinary women—need each other. Being extraordinary only takes you so far. Only when women come together do patterns become clear; only by comparing notes do a series of individual decisions become an instance of collective discrimination. It is only by collecting these experiences that individual women, even the most extraordinary, have the opportunity to fulfill their potential.

Had three women not gotten together, the MIT study would never have begun. Those three women, as the report makes clear, did not believe that they had been discriminated against until they talked to one another. Feminists have been roundly criticized, by female and male critics, for turning women into victims, but the greater danger may be how many of us are determined not to see ourselves in that light, even if it is true.

When I first started teaching law, I resisted teaching the course on gender discrimination (it was then called "women and the law") out of fear that it would brand me as "one of them"—that I wouldn't be taken seriously, accepted in the tribe, given tenure. But I have learned an important lesson along the way, one that has led me to teach gender discrimination for the last decade or more: If that's the way they see the world, they'll see you that way, too, no matter what you do.

You can do your best to prove just how extraordinary you are as a manager, professor, lawyer, or board member; do all the hard stuff; try to beat them at their own game, without reminding them, ever, that you're really a woman. You can put off the mastectomy, move to Chicago, leave your baby with the in-laws. You can truly be extraordinary. And by and large, it still doesn't work. They still look at you and what they see is a woman—granted, better than the rest, tolerable even—but still a woman, with all that has traditionally implied.

THREE

Equal Under the Law

When I was in law school, if you were a liberal, the most sought-after clerkships in the country were Wright and Brennan. Wright was Judge J. Skelly Wright of the United States Court of Appeals for the D.C. Circuit, the most powerful court, particularly in the more activist days, and one of the most courageous, decent men ever to serve as a judge. Brennan was Justice William Brennan, the court's leading liberal, a close friend of Wright's, who generally hired Judge Wright's Harvard clerk (usually the president of the *Harvard Law Review*) without meeting them. Judge Wright hired without regard to race or gender: He just wanted the top student in the class at both Harvard and Yale. When I applied to work for him, he'd only had one female clerk, Sally Katzen, now one of Washington's premier lawyers. That made me nervous. But he hired me, sight unseen, the day he got my resumé, which was the day I sent it, as arranged by a former clerk and now professor, the way it always was.

A year later, on my first day of work, Judge Wright took me into his chambers to explain that I shouldn't take it personally, but Justice Brennan had decided to hire my co-clerk, a University of Chicago alumnus, to work for him the next year, sight unseen. He had always picked Harvard over Chicago. He'd gone to Harvard. He'd never even met me before deciding to make an exception that year. But I shouldn't take it personally, the judge told me. It was because I was a woman.

I couldn't believe my ears. The most liberal member of the court, the most articulate opponent of sex discrimination, wouldn't hire me because I was a woman. Who do you complain to? I'd heard the story of the lone woman who had worked for the justice some years ago, the daughter of a family friend. She wasn't really a clerk; she later committed suicide. But that wasn't the reason, the judge assured me, that his friend wouldn't hire me. He said his chambers worked better when it was the justice and the "boys." Judge Wright thought it was really about his secretary, who liked to be the only woman in the office. (Some years later, the justice's wife died, he married his secretary, and started hiring women clerks.)

I did take it personally. Being a woman is personal and immutable, which is what makes it an inappropriate basis for making decisions about who gets what in our society. But at least I knew what I was up against. I didn't go home and worry about whether it was my low grade in Property my first year, or something about my resumé or my cover letter, or a supporter who was secretly criticizing me behind my back. The discrimination I confronted as a young woman was explicit and unmistakable. In a way, that made it easier. The question was not why you didn't get hired, but whether the justification for the discrimination was a legally sufficient one.

It was not until 1972 that the Supreme Court of the United States first recognized that the equal protection of the laws guaranteed by the United States Constitution extended to women. For two centuries, the Court had enforced laws dividing the world into separate spheres for men and women. Men ran the public sphere, where laws were made and property changed hands and wars were waged; women raised the families and tended to the home front. The two worlds were both separate and unequal. What changed over these two hundred years was not this sexual asymmetry that we think of as discrimination, but the justification offered to support it.

In the nineteenth century, it was "the divine law of the Creator," in the words of one justice of the United States, that the state of Illinois be permitted to bar Myra Bradwell from the practice of law because she was a woman. As Justice Bradley put it, writing for himself and two other members of the Court:

> The civil law, as well as nature herself, has always recognized a wide difference in the respective spheres and destinies of man and woman. Man is, or should be, woman's protector and defender. The natural and proper timidity and delicacy which belongs to the female sex evidently unfits it for many of the occupations of civil life. The constitution of the family organization, which is founded in the divine ordinance, as well as in the nature of things, indicates the domestic sphere as that which properly belongs to the domain and functions of womanhood.

Of course, not all women had husbands—who could own all their property—and children, who could occupy all their energies. But in the ideology of separate spheres, women who were different were legally invisible. To quote Justice Bradley again:

> It is true that many women are unmarried and not affected by any of the duties, complications, and incapacities arising out of the married state, but these are exceptions to the general rule. The paramount destiny and mission of woman are to fulfil the noble and benign offices of wife and mother. This is the law of the Creator. And the rules of civil society must be adapted to the general constitution of things, and cannot be based upon exceptional cases.

In other words, women are to be viewed as wives and mothers, whether or not they are. Those who defy the norm are, as a matter of law, invisible.

By the turn of the century, it was science and sociology, rather than divine law, which was invoked by courts to justify the legal enforcement of separate spheres. A 1908 Oregon law restricting hours of work for women, but not for men, was upheld by the United States Supreme Court on the grounds that women are, quite simply, different from men in ways that make them less able to work:

> That woman's physical structure and the performance of maternal functions place her at a disadvantage in the struggle for subsistence is obvious. This is especially true when the burdens of motherhood are upon her. Even when they are not, by abundant testimony of the medical fraternity, continuance for a long time on her feet at work repeating this from day to day, tends to injurious effects upon the body, and as healthy mothers are essential to vigorous offspring, the physical well-being of woman becomes an object of public interest and care in order to preserve the strength and vigor of the race.

What defines a woman, in the scientific view, is her reproductive capacity. All women are created to be mothers; to defy gender expectations, by choice or not, is to be invisible as a matter of law. It is, of course, precisely the same view taken by Justice Bradley for divine reasons.

During World War II, women—notwithstanding their "physical structure and the performance of maternal functions"—stepped into men's roles to keep the domestic economy producing the necessities of war. Neither science nor sociology stood in the way of Rosie the Riveter, which forced the Supreme Court to find a new basis for postwar restrictions on women's employment: deference to the legislative majority.

Under Michigan law in the 1940s, women were allowed to work as waitresses in taverns, but not as bartenders. An exception was provided, however, for the wives and daughters of male tavern owners. Justice Frankfurter, writing for the majority, which upheld the law, considered it "beyond question" that Michigan could forbid all women from working behind a bar. The exception provided a knottier problem: If bartending was, in the legislature's judgment, incompatible with femalehood, what difference did it make who you were related to? Michigan, the court concluded, "evidently believes that the oversight assured through ownership of a bar by a barmaid's husband or father minimizes hazards that may confront a barmaid without such protective oversight. This Court is certainly not in a position to gainsay such belief by the Michigan legislature."

What is so striking about the Michigan statute, of course, is that waitresses may be subject to the same "hazards" as bar-

tenders—only they make less money for their troubles. I bar-
tended my way through law school not only because it paid
better than waitressing, which I had done in high school and
college, but because the barrier of a big wooden structure
(the bar) and the power to decide who drank actually made it
a much better job for a woman than bending over men to
serve drinks. What the all-male Michigan legislature was also
protecting was the wallets of men. The public world has
never really been closed to women; only its greatest rewards
have been.

In 1954, the United States Supreme Court in the landmark case of *Brown v. Board of Education* held that, in matters
of race, separate but equal is inherently unequal. But not so in
matters of sex.

Seven years after *Brown*, a Florida woman challenged her
conviction for the second-degree murder of her husband. In
nineties' parlance, Mrs. Hoyt was an abused spouse. She killed
her husband by hitting him with a baseball bat during a fight
in which she claimed that he insulted and humiliated her. Her
defense was temporary insanity; her claim was that women
might understand her situation better than men did. Under
Florida law, both men and women could serve on juries, but
men were automatically placed on the rolls for service,

whereas women had to register with the clerk of courts and thus affirmatively take steps evincing their desire to be placed on the jury list. Not surprisingly, the result was that men served on juries far more often than women did. Mrs. Hoyt was convicted by an all-male jury.

The United States Supreme Court upheld Hoyt's conviction, reasoning that "despite the enlightened emancipation of women from the restrictions and protections of bygone years, and their entry into many parts of community life formerly considered to be reserved to men, woman is still regarded as the center of home and family life." Therefore, Florida was justified in enforcing different rules for jury service.

The legislative decision to which the Court was deferring in *Hoyt* was grounded quite explicitly in the ideology of separate spheres for men and women. As the state argued in its brief to the Court:

The rearing of children, even if it be conceded that the socio-psychologists have made inroads thereon, nevertheless remains a prime responsibility of the matriarch. The home, though it no longer be the log cabin in the wilderness, must nevertheless be maintained. The advent of "T.V." dinners does not remove the burden of providing palatable food for the members of the family, the husband is still, in the main, the breadwinner, child's hurts are almost without exception, bound and treated by the mother.

Hoyt is the background for the battles that came later; every feminist lawyer above a certain age can recite *Hoyt*. Women, in the ideology of *Hoyt*, are seen only as wives and mothers. If the woman is a physician, she is not treated the way a male physician is (required to register, but automatically subject to being excused) but like a mother. If the woman is unmarried and has no children, she is still treated as a mother. All other roles, all other women, are legally invisible.

Worse still, while women are sufficiently different from men, as a group, to justify separate rules, they are also sufficiently unimportant that their participation in a jury—the essence of citizen responsibility in the public sphere—is entirely unnecessary. That is the cruelest irony of *Hoyt*. If women and men are interchangeable for purposes of jury service, wouldn't that argue that the same rules must apply? If women are so different, as Florida believed and the Supreme Court agreed, shouldn't that argue that a jury system that excludes them cannot fairly apportion guilt or innocence?

The message of *Hoyt* is clear: Women belong in the private sphere; biology is destiny, whether you follow your destiny or not; in the public sphere, women are neither the same as, nor are they equal to, men, nor is their voice needed in making judgments or shaping rules.

It was not until *Reed v. Reed*, decided in 1972, that the Supreme Court for the first time held otherwise. *Reed* involved an Idaho law that provided that in any contest between two equally related candidates to be the administrator of a will, the man should win. Administrative convenience was cited by the state as a reason. The Court rejected that explanation, holding the statute unconstitutional.

In cases challenging racial classifications, the Court had come to apply a standard of scrutiny, which was strict in theory and generally fatal in fact. Race was deemed a suspect basis for government to draw lines among people. The reason for the enhanced scrutiny, the Court repeatedly explained, was the danger faced by "discrete and insular minorities," particularly those who have traditionally been the victims of discrimination, and whose rights would not necessarily be protected in the political process. Chief Justice Earl Warren, who lead the Court in articulating this level of racial scrutiny, used to say that if the cases guaranteeing blacks equal representation in the political process had been decided earlier, *Brown v. Board of Education* itself might have been unnecessary; that is how strongly he saw the connection between the failures of the political process and the obligation to afford strict scrutiny.

Women's advocates, lead by Ruth Bader Ginsburg, now a justice on the Supreme Court, argued that sex should be treated the same as race, for purposes of enhanced scrutiny. But that position never commanded five votes; race and sex are not the same, in the law or in practice. Instead, in constitutional cases, the Court articulated a middle level of scrutiny, requiring defenders of gender lines to bear the burden of showing that they served a very important, if not compelling, government interest. But feminists still won virtually every case they brought, eliminating gender lines in the social security laws, military dependents benefits, alimony, jury selection, drinking age, and pension benefits. In the eyes of the law, men and women were to be treated the same.

The Constitution and the Bill of Rights only apply to "state action," preventing lawmakers, or public employers, from drawing lines based on race and gender, but leaving the private sector free to do whatever it wanted. In 1963, Congress passed the Equal Pay Act, which mandated that women who did the same jobs as men in the private sector must be paid the same amount for doing them. The Equal Pay Act was an important step forward, but it sounds more radical than it was, particularly in context. In 1963, and even today, women don't do the same jobs as men. That is the problem.

The Civil Rights Act, enacted in 1964 against the opposition of mostly Southerners who claimed that it invaded states' rights and private freedom, prohibited discrimination on the basis of race, religion, or national origin in employment, housing, and public accommodations. As a last-minute effort to defeat the bill, opponents added sex to Title VII's prohibition of employment discrimination. The amendment was intended to underscore the foolhardiness of the enterprise: Who, after all, would oppose sex discrimination in employment? Congress passed the bill anyway, which is why there is no legislative history of the inclusion of sex. The feminist revolution in the workplace owes its start, in part, to its most unenlightened opponents.

Notwithstanding its origin, the courts have taken seriously Title VII's prohibitions of sex-based employment discrimination. Those who sought to enforce gender lines—whether it has been the airlines or fire and police departments—have been forced to defend them as bona-fide occupational qualifications. Height and weight restrictions, which operate to exclude women in practice if not explicitly, must be shown to be a business necessity. Eliminating subgroups of women—all mothers of preschool children, for example—while allowing other women to work, has been prohibited as "sex plus" discrimination. The fact that male passengers might prefer, or feel more comfortable with, female flight attendants is not enough to justify the exclusion of men from that occupation given that the primary purpose of flight attendants is the safety of passengers, which involves tasks men are equally capable of performing.

The common thrust of these efforts, both constitutional and statutory, was that the law, and employers, had to treat men and women the same. The rule for men must be the same rule for women.

That this was not always good for women, at least in the most immediate and practical sense, was apparent from the beginning. Some of the laws that feminists attacked provided extra benefits for women, not extra burdens: presumptions in their favor in custody decisions; automatic health coverage when their husbands served in the military. As a matter of law, then Justice Rehnquist argued, why give extra scrutiny to laws which disadvantage men, who are hardly a discrete and insular minority unable to protect themselves in the political process?

As a matter of politics, Phyllis Schlafly argued, why should women support a movement that would strip them of the protections the law gives them, treating them as if they were just like men when it's perfectly clear that most women aren't? Feminism, she argued, pitted the women who were headed for the public sector against the wives and mothers at home, the women against the ladies, and took the side of the former.

The feminist answer was that any gender-based line, even one that seemed to help women, inevitably reinforced the very stereotypes that served to limit individual freedom for both men and women. As Justice Brennan put it, in striking down a law that provided automatic dependency benefits to the wives of servicemen but required the husbands of service-women to prove their dependency, the attitude of "romantic paternalism," which was invoked to rationalize discrimination that supposedly protected women, "in practical effect put women not on a pedestal but in a cage." One of the cases feminists were most proud of, one that Justice Ginsburg still invokes, was *Weinberger v. Weisenfeld*, a 1975 lawsuit on behalf of a father who wanted to stay home and raise the children after his wife died, but was denied the social security benefits that would have gone to a surviving wife and mother in those circumstances. The idea of feminist law reform was to allow women to cross into the public sphere and men into the private sphere on the same terms, to end the enforcement of stereotypes by law and the punishment of those who deviate from them. Men could be parents; not all women had to be.

The political problems created by this stance were, as Sheila Tobias has eloquently acknowledged in *Faces of Feminism,* well-exploited by Phyllis Shlafly and conservative Republicans. Enforcing equality in an unequal world doesn't produce equal results. Even the Supreme Court occasionally would ignore its own assaults on inequality and wink at tax benefits for widows, or phase in changes in social security rules that had favored women. In the world, most of the traffic was in one direction: The case of a man staying home with the children was and is still exceptional, while women were rushing, or being pushed, into the public world, albeit mostly to the same low-paying jobs that have always been considered women's work. Law reformers obviously could see this; in academics, critical legal studies had become the discourse for feminist theory, while the work of Carol Gilligan and others on the differences between girls and boys was being celebrated by many self-defined cultural feminists.

.   .   .

No case better captured the cleavage within feminisms, much less within the larger population of women, than the issue of how the law should deal with pregnancy. In 1976, the nine men of the Supreme Court had concluded that distinctions based on pregnancy did not amount to sex discrimination; not all women get pregnant, the Court noted accurately, in contrast to so many earlier cases where it seemed to forget that; as a result, the class of persons advantaged by the practice of providing comprehensive disability coverage for every disability but pregnancy was comprised of both men and women. To be sure. But the class disadvantaged was comprised entirely of women, and only women, pregnancy being the one difference between men and women not subject to the nature versus nurture debate.

The decisions, applied both in constitutional and statutory cases, produced an unusually broad consensus for legislative reversal in Congress. Everyone is for pregnancy; it unites left and right, one of the few occasions where the choice divide can be avoided. So Congress overwhelmingly passed the Pregnancy Discrimination Act of 1978, which was intended to overrule these Court decisions at least so far as Title VII of the Civil Rights Act was concerned. By its terms, it specifically prohibited employers from treating pregnancy differently than any other disability. No special rules for pregnancy. The statute could not be more explicit.

Or so California Federal Bank argued in 1987, in claiming that compliance with a new California statute requiring employers to provide unpaid maternity would force the bank to violate Title VII. Liberal feminists agreed. I was on the National Board of the American Civil Liberties Union at the time. The case was on its way to the Supreme Court. The Southern California chapter was in favor of the statute; the national board, after hearing them out, voted to take the other side. The same debate was repeated in liberal and feminist organizations across America.

What were liberals doing arguing *against* a state law that would make it easier for women to keep their jobs after giving birth to a child? What were feminists doing opposing what was clearly seen as a benefit that women wanted and needed?

Some claimed that pregnancy benefits weren't really a benefit after all. Requiring employers to give unpaid leave to mothers would discourage them from hiring women in the first instance, making it too expensive, adding a cost to women workers, giving them one more reason to prefer the man. But no one was opposed to unpaid parenting leave, even though it was understood that women would be the ones who took it most often. It wasn't the cost argument that motivated the nation's leading legal feminists to oppose the California approach. It was fear, backed by history. We had been brought up to understand that it was women's reproductive capacity that defined them as a matter of law and limited their ability to participate on equal terms in the public sphere. How could we allow a line to be drawn based on pregnancy, even one that seemed to help women? Maybe this time it would help, but what about next time? I remember my friend Nadine Strossen, now the American Civil Liberties Union's first female president, taking me aside, armed with a stack of letters from all the legal luminaries: Herma Hill Kay, Wendy Williams, Eleanor Holmes Norton. "You can't trust them," she argued, meaning the men in the courts, judges. "It won't be us drawing the lines, but men in power; it will be used against us; it will make it more difficult, not less, to beat them at their own game." That was the business we were in. I agreed.

The Supreme Court ultimately did something that never occurred to most of us. They upheld the California statute, even though it plainly violated the words of Title VII. They refused to buy into the either-or choice that seemed to confront the rest of us. They refused to be bound by a plain meaning that made no sense. This wasn't the sort of "discrimination" Congress had in mind, even if the words of the statutes technically prohibited it. Employers, they said, were prohibited from discriminating on the basis of pregnancy in the terms and conditions of employment, but they could be required to grant pregnancy leave.

By the tenets of the legal process, courts aren't supposed to do that; even the Supreme Court is supposed to interpret federal statutes, not rewrite them. But almost no one complained. Congress certainly wasn't about to overrule them. Civil rights groups, divided internally, pronounced the divisions solved by the Court's brilliant resolution. It may not be the way the system is supposed to work, but there is an important lesson in that for feminists nonetheless: Sometimes the only stance that makes sense is to refuse to accept the choices placed in front of you; to opt to rewrite the question, rather than answer the one posed.

FOUR

The Facts of Life

The day after the government granted its approval to the megamerger of America Online and Time Warner in 2000, the new organizational chart was released. At the time of the merger, it had been announced that AOL's Steve Case would head the new company with Time Warner's Gerald Levin right below him. But how the two companies would be combined and who would end up running what was the subject of speculation well beyond the offices of those directly affected. As it should be: Control over both content and access at this level puts enormous power in very few hands. The big story was that the companies were going to divide between content and distribution, with separate reporting lines. The organizational roster was laid out in the *New York Times* with twenty-four names listed. Not one of them was a woman's. Not one. It was not mentioned in the article. It is not news that men are in charge.

In 1978, futurologist Herman Kahn was asked how many years it would be before 25 percent of the CEOs of Fortune 500 companies were women. "About two thousand years," he said. "But make it 10 percent, and I'll say within twenty years." Business magazines were making similar predictions; in 1976, *Business Week* identified one hundred corporate women and predicted that a number of them were on their way to the top jobs in their companies. But Kahn was wrong, and so was *Business Week,* which ten years later was making new lists that also turned out to be wrong.

I understand that women have made progress, and I don't mean to suggest otherwise. I am extremely grateful to the women and men who opened doors for me. But those who think that "the problem" is solved, or that time will solve it, will have a very hard time explaining these numbers. That is my purpose. My goal is not to prove how far women have come, but how far we have to go; my aim is not to make us pat one another on the back, but to shock the complacent who think feminism is unnecessary in the twenty-first century.

I recognize that this is, in some respects, a dangerous enterprise. Whatever study I cite will be attacked by someone somewhere for its methodology, timeliness, the breadth of the sample, the reliability of the authors, and the like. Not so, they will cry, fearing what women might do if they actually knew where they stood. Look what you've ignored! others will exclaim, pointing out that women do better in small business than in big business, in the nonprofit world rather than in the for-profit sector.

My interest in trying to describe the status quo is not to engage in a war of factoids. Let's hope that by the time this book is published, there will be 10 women and 490 men running Fortune 500 corporations, instead of the 3 women and 497 men there are now. Maybe the rate at which women are promoted to partner in major New York law firms will rise above 5 percent, and the number of major American companies with no women or one woman on their boards will decline. Maybe there will be 75 women in the top 2,500 earners in the Fortune 500, or even 100, instead of the 63 the Catalyst study found last year.

Nor is it my intent to diminish the accomplishments of women who have left big business for small business, left big law firms for small ones, left corporate America for the high-tech or the not-for-profit sector. But too many of those women left because they couldn't find a way to use their talents in the corporate world, or couldn't find a way back in. And as important as small business is, the corporate giants wield power not only over the people who work for them but also over the nations in which they do business.

There are lots of reasons that any individual, male or female, doesn't reach the top of his or her profession. They may lack the skills, the ability, even the luck. They may be lousy politicians, or not care enough, or not want it badly enough. But those are traits one would expect to find, if it's an equal world and a level playing field, in both men and women. It's true that not all men succeed. But some do. On a percentage basis, it's rather stunning. Twenty-five years ago, graduating business school classes included 20 to 25 percent women; today, 99.94 percent of the CEOs, and 97.3 percent of the top earners are men. That is not what a random distribution of success looks like by any measure.

In 1978, Katharine Graham was the only female CEO of a Fortune 500 company. After the death of her husband, she took over the *Washington Post,* which had been run first by her father and then by her husband. When she retired in 1991, she was one of two female CEOs. As of 1999, there are three women running Fortune 500 companies—not 10 percent, not even 5 percent, but less than one-half of 1 percent. When *Business Week* went back ten years later to its top one hundred women of 1976, it found that its earlier optimism was "overblown"; of the one hundred, "many are sticking it out, though resigned to the idea that they may advance—but never to the highest corporate offices. Others have abandoned big companies to start their own businesses, new careers, or families." Only one of the one hundred made it onto *Business Week*'s 1987 list of fifty, a group that the magazine claimed at the time was "vastly different" than the earlier list—"better educated, more single-minded, and more confident about their prospects." Different though they may have been, only one woman from that list has since made it to the top.

Not many more women can be found in the number two, three, four, or five positions in large corporations. A 1998 study by Catalyst examined the sex of those holding the top five positions in every Fortune 500 company. Catalyst found that only 63 women held positions in the highest ranks of corporate America, compared to 2,373 men. These 63 women represent just 2.4 percent of the 2,430 corporate officers holding titles of chairman, vice chairman, chief executive officer, president, chief operating officer, and executive vice president. More broadly, of the 978 women holding a vice president–level title (less than 10 percent of the total sample), only 28 percent held positions with profit-and-loss or revenue-generating responsibility, generally considered a prerequisite to make it to the top in corporate America. And corporate women earn less than men. Another study from Catalyst, also from 1998, found corporate women earning almost one-third less than men of similar rank.

On Wall Street, as of 1996, only 8 percent of the managing directors of investment and brokerage houses were women. As of 1998, only 8 percent of the partners in Big 5 accounting firms were women. In November 1998, *Worth* magazine's compilation of the twenty most powerful "players" on Wall Street included nineteen men and one woman, analyst Abby Joseph Cohen; among the out-of-town players, ten of ten were white men. Even more tellingly, the ten hottest up-and-comers, the oldest of whom was forty-seven, were all white men.

The pattern is similar in the legal profession. According to a 1998 study by the *National Law Journal,* 13.6 percent of the partners in the nation's 250 largest law firms were women, while 86.4 percent were men; and of the women who are partners, only 54 percent were equity partners, who share in the profits, compared to 74 percent of the male partners. Moreover, the promotion rate for women from associate status to positions as partners may actually be decreasing. A 1995 study of eight major law firms for the New York City Bar Association by respected researcher Cynthia Fuchs Epstein (cited in the American Bar Association's study of women in the profession, aptly entitled "Overcoming the Sisyphus Factor") found that for those associates hired between 1973 and 1981, 21 percent of the men and 15 percent of the women attained partnership. Promotion rates for those hired after 1981 declined for both men and women, reflecting the effect of the economic downturn. But the decrease was far greater for women: among post-1981 hires, 17 percent of the male associates and only 5 percent of the female associates were promoted to partner. A study done by the ABA in 1991 found that among lawyers who entered practice after 1967, 18 percent of the women had become partners compared to 45 percent of the men.

What is equally troubling, the American Bar Association found in its landmark study, is that younger women, looking at the sacrifices made by women of my generation to make partner and get ahead, increasingly want none of it; they "understand" that a choice must be made between success at work and family life, and they are willing to make it, in favor of family. The problem is not that they are making the wrong choice, but that they see it as inevitable, and the provision of options like "of counsel" makes it even easier to opt out of the rat race. Unfortunately, that decision tends to have lasting consequences.

Meanwhile, the law firms themselves are eager to avoid any suggestion that they are trying to promote women, or offering them any flexibility or opportunities not available to men. In presenting the results of the 1998 partnership promotions, *Of Counsel,* a legal publication, points out: "Interestingly, law firm managers these days seem at least as anxious to emphasize the extent to which they don't favor women as they are to point out how gender-friendly their firm cultures have become. It's no doubt a reflection on the competitive milieu in which law firms operate that there's no worse fate than a perception among clients that they've lowered partnership admission standards. From a business standpoint, they'd be better off branded as sexists."

In Hollywood, the hottest agency of the moment,

Endeavor, is a partnership of ten white men, all of them under forty-five. A recent portrait in the *Los Angeles Times* shows the ten of them gathered around the conference table, smiling. The percentage of women working as writers and directors in Hollywood has been flat for ten years, even though this is an industry dominated by younger artists. Indeed, a study by Women in Film of women working on a TV series found that the number for the 1997–98 season was actually lower than it had been two years before, putting female employment below the percentage of female guild members. In the movies, male writers outnumber female writers five to one. When it comes to directing, 93.2 percent of the jobs go to men.

In academia, men publish more than women, hold higher ranks, and earn more money than women with equal experience. As Dr. Susan Blumenthal, the ranking female doctor in the government, argues, the same pattern holds in medicine; more women are entering the profession, but the deans and department chairmen, and the highest earners, remain overwhelmingly male. While 43 percent of new entrants into medicine are female, and 26 percent of all faculty members are female, the numbers at the top are entirely different: 7 percent of the deans, 6.5 percent of the department chairs, and 11 percent of the full professors are women. What makes these numbers particularly striking is that women have been going to medical school in significant numbers for twenty-five years (in 1974, 22 percent of the new entrants were women; in 1984, nearly 30 percent of the graduates were), but they are not penetrating the top ranks even when men of that generation are.

Women do better in small businesses than in large ones; better in entrepreneurial efforts than in corporate ones. But even here, men are dominant. *Inc.* magazine's list of the top one hundred entrepreneurial firms in 1997 included only one headed by a woman; it took ten years to get from zero to one. A 1999 survey by the Information Technology Association of America found that women accounted for 41 percent of the employees in that field, mostly in lower-paying administrative jobs, while men accounted for close to 75 percent of the well-paying positions. Women make up 7 percent of the officers in high-tech companies, which is actually lower than the number for all Fortune 500 firms. The wage gap at the top in high tech—sixty-eight cents on the dollar—is actually wider than the overall wage gap.

The situation for minority women is worse still. When people speak of women making inroads in corporate America, they almost always mean white women. A 1999 Catalyst survey of 1,735 women of color from thirty leading U.S. companies found that women of color were twice as likely as white women to believe that there had been no progress at all in their advancement opportunities, that a majority thought existing diversity programs to be totally ineffective, and that the appropriate metaphor for minority managers was not a glass ceiling, but a concrete barrier, which leaves even the highest-ranking minority women unable to imagine the possibility of change.

The majority of women who work continue to be employed in the same sex–segregated categories that women have always dominated. Professor Vicki Schultz estimates that 60 percent of the workforce would have to change jobs to balance occupational categories by gender. While the wage gap has narrowed since the days of fifty-nine cents on the dollar, it has not closed; indeed, in recent years, it has actually grown a bit. Currently, working women as a group earn about seventy-two cents for every dollar men earn. What's worse, behind the declining wage-gap figures is the painful reality that Professor Victor Fuchs outlines in his 1998 book, *Women's Quest for Economic Equality:* "Women had less leisure while men had more, an increase in the proportion of adults not married made more women dependent on their own income, and women's share of financial responsibility for children rose."

Those women who do enter traditionally male fields find themselves working almost exclusively for men in cultures defined by male norms. A recent study by the International Association of Chiefs of Police found that women have won more than one-third of the sexual harassment cases they have filed against local police departments. That is an extraordinarily high number. In explaining these results, Joseph D. McNamara, the progressive former chief of the San Jose Police Department and currently a research fellow at Stanford University's Hoover Institution, points specifically to the absence of women in top positions. According to studies by the Chiefs Association, 91 percent of the departments have no women in policy-making positions; only 123 of the 17,000 police agencies in the country have women as chiefs; and only 12 percent of the police officers in the country are women, a number that hasn't gone up in the last ten years. Put another way, 16,877 of the 17,000 chiefs, and 88 percent of the officers who work for them, are men. Yet in lawsuit after lawsuit, departments have been unable to validate height and weight requirements as necessary to do the job of policing; indeed, the Christopher Commission, which studied police practices in the aftermath of the 1992 Los Angeles riots, actually found that female officers may be more effective than their male counterparts in defusing potentially violent situations without resorting to the use of force.

In 1956, sociologist C. Wright Mills set about to study who wielded power in America, defining and examining the leaders of the military-industrial establishment in this country. The major hypothesis Mills was testing was the popular myth that this had become a country of Horatio Algers, of powerful men who rose from meager backgrounds to wield positions of power. In fact, it wasn't: The "power elite," as Mills termed it, turned out to be white, Protestant, male, and overwhelmingly privileged in its socioeconomic background.

Retracing Mills's steps four decades later, psychologist Richard L. Zweigenhaft and sociologist G. William Domhoff, the latter among the most respected and senior men in the field and the author of the seminal *Who Rules America?* sought to determine the extent to which Mills's power elite has become diversified in terms of race, gender, ethnicity, and class. Of all the groups they studied, only Jews have penetrated the power elite in numbers sufficient to represent their share of the population. But even that is somewhat misleading: Proportionately, more Jews attend elite educational institutions than make it to the corporate boardrooms; the Jews who do are more likely to have married non-Jewish women and have assimilated into the Protestant culture. The power elite remains overwhelmingly white, male, and Protestant, even though individual women, blacks, and Hispanics have gained entrée.

In examining women in the corporate power elite, Zweigenhaft and Domhoff point out that the greatest progress has been made in the representation of women on corporate boards, particularly since Catalyst began doing an annual survey and widely publicizing its results. In 1977, in its first count, Catalyst found that there were a total of 46 women on the boards of the 1,300 largest companies in America, which amounted to well under 1 percent. Seven years later, Catalyst counted again, and the number had gone up to 367, or 2.3 percent of all the directors. Beginning in 1993, Catalyst decided to count every year as a way to draw attention to the absence of women on corporate boards.

"The day we began the 1994 count," Catalyst president Sheila Wellington wrote, in explaining their theory, "the fax began a steady six-week hum, with company after company telling of their new women directors." In the ten years from 1984 to 1994, the percentage of directorships held by women rose from just over 2 percent to 6.9 percent; in 1996, Catalyst found that the number exceeded 10 percent for the first time, though the rate of increase had begun to decline. Only 188 of the Fortune 500 have more than one woman on their boards; 312 companies have either one or none.

Even more important, the number of women serving as "inside directors" remains stunningly low: 1.1 percent as of 1998. It is the inside directors who run the company; it is the inside directors who generally form the pool of candidates for CEO jobs, both in their own companies and in others. And that pool is 99 percent male.

Even when they are represented on corporate boards and in top management, women may not serve the same functions as men. According to a study by Diana Bilimoria and Sandy Kristin Piderit in which they controlled for work experience, male directors are more likely than their female peers to serve on the compensation, executive, and finance committees of the board, while female directors are more likely than their male peers to serve on the public affairs committee. Men serve on the powerful committees; women on the less powerful ones.

Zweigenhaft and Domhoff go a step further. They conclude that women in corporations are there not only to create an appearance of diversity and to deflect criticism from the female family members of the men who own and run them, "but to provide a valuable buffer between the men who control the corporation and the corporation's labor force and the general public." Of the women who held titles of vice president or above in 1996, only 28 percent were in positions with operational responsibility for profit and loss; men are more likely to hold line positions, while women tend to be concentrated in the "velvet ghettos" of public relations and labor relations. In this sense, women provide the buffer between the men of their own class and the men of the class below; and because such "staff" jobs, vital though they are to the men in power, are not themselves considered a route to power, "women end up playing an increasingly important role in corporations without gaining increasing power." Buffers neither make it to the top, nor make the rules; they enforce the rules that exist, made by others.

Equally telling is the fact that the very few women who do make it to the top make less than their male counterparts, taking all factors into account. Professor Virginia Valian explained her findings in her recent book, *Why So Slow,* that not only do women at universities and colleges have lower average salaries than men at every rank, but the inequalities are progressive: the higher your rank, the greater the disparity. Professor Valian compared the pay scales at elite universities with those at all universities, and found that the pay gap persisted. She compared the data by discipline, testing the theory that it is because there are more men in science and mathematics, for instance, and found that women earn less than men in almost every field, particularly at the highest ranks. The only exception was for women's schools—a very small minority of all educational institutions—which pay women full professors equally to men, in contrast to private coeducational schools, which pay women 88 percent of a man's salary.

Similarly, a 1991 study of 502 men and women who received MBA degrees from one of the top ten business schools in the United States between 1976 and 1986 found not only that the women earned less than the men, but that the gap remained even when the researchers controlled for the type of position, starting salary, experience, age, job performance, and type of industry.

In engineering, where qualifications tend to be both standardized and similar for men and women, the same disparities can be found. In a study of male and female engineering graduates, researchers found that women tended to be over-represented in the lower prestige and lower paying ranks, while men were overrepresented at the top, and that women tended to move backward—from high prestige to low prestige—at ten times the rate men did; 22 percent of the women in the study, compared to 2 percent of the men, were downwardly mobile, professionally speaking.

In 1998, as noted earlier, Catalyst found only sixty-three women among the top five earners in each of the Fortune 500 companies, a universe that, taking account of vacancies and duplications, came to 2,320 people. Even within this rarified group, there is a pay gap between men and women that cannot be eliminated by controlling for age and experience, does not go away even when the 99.6 percent male cohort of CEOs is excluded, and doesn't disappear when differences between the valuations of line and staff jobs are taken into account. As Sheila Wellington pointed out in the *Wall Street Journal,* responding to the conservative attack by two female scholars from the American Enterprise Institute, female top earners who have line responsibilities not only make less than male top earners with line jobs, they make less than the men in the group who have staff jobs. Or to quote one management consultant who wrote to defend the Catalyst study, "put a female name at the top of a man's resumé and watch the value go down."

In my house, there's one word that commands immediate attention and respect. Or rather, one name: Reveta. Reveta Bowers is the head of the independent school my children have attended since they were toddlers. It is a wonderful and much sought after school in Los Angeles, a city where entertainment is a dominant industry. It could be all celebrities, but it isn't, because Reveta wouldn't let it be. No one gets to be a celebrity at school. We all work at the fair, phone calls get returned in the order received, and the list of famous people who have not gotten their kids in is as long as the list of the ones who have. Diversity is valued far more than celebrity. It is a remarkable school, and no one doubts that the most important reason why is Reveta. When, a few years ago, a former student of mine asked me who Vice President Gore should have dinner with on his night off from media and money people, the first name I gave her was Reveta's.

You get to see what a person's made of when they run your kids' school. Some years ago, Disney chairman Michael Eisner's children attended the school, and he got to watch Reveta, and came away with the same impression of her that most parents have. Sheer awe. More than a decade after the youngest Eisner child moved on to middle school, Reveta Bowers was elected to the board of the Walt Disney Company.

I thought it was a brilliant choice. When a high school class studying social action wrote to me about the fact that Disneyland assigned attendants to certain rides based on sex, with boys working on the jungle cruise and girls working on the fairy-tale ride, I gave their letter right to Reveta. It turns out the official explanation was that they didn't have the right size uniforms, but pity the poor person who tried to convince Reveta that uniform size justifies sex discrimination. Abracadabra, there were new uniforms, and the students who brought about this change got a free trip to Disneyland.

Every year, TIAA-CREF, the giant pension fund, challenges Reveta's reelection to the Disney Board. It is done publicly at the shareholders' meeting. They cast their votes against her, as do some other pension funds that have followed their lead on the grounds that she is insufficiently independent. TIAA-CREF is the pension fund for teachers and educators. It is her pension fund, and they vote against her anyway.

In all of my research, I have found no instance where a CEO has gotten in trouble for turning to someone he plays golf or tennis with, or sees at an exclusive club, or socializes with on weekends. I have found no claims that knowing someone from prep school days disqualifies them from serving as an independent director. When old boys are challenged, which is rare, there's always a financial interest cited. School ties are just fine.

Reveta Bowers grew up in South Central Los Angeles, attended the University of Southern California on scholarship, and began her career as a kindergarten teacher in the Los Angeles Unified School District. She is the only African-American woman on the Disney board, and the only elementary school educator. Women of color comprise 1 percent of the board members in the 700-plus corporations surveyed by Catalyst last year. Reveta is one of fewer than one hundred female board members. You'd think her election would be cause for celebration, not an occasion for an annual humiliation. They did it again this year. But she still loves the work she does on the board. Does she make a difference? How could she not? Everyone behaves when Reveta is around. Even grown-ups.

FIVE

Motherhood as

Destiny

You can have two out of three, Paramount chief Sherry Lansing once told a reporter. Take your choice: husband; kids; top job. If you pick kids, your chances of the top job go way down.

More mothers are working than ever before, and they are working longer hours than ever before. Being a mother does not mean that you don't work; the majority of mothers, even in married, two-parent families, work. What it means is that you are likely to earn less, be promoted less often, and be viewed—and even see yourself—as a less valuable, more costly worker.

By some measures, this may be true. Most working mothers are probably not willing to leave their infants with in-laws and commute two thousand miles every week. We don't want to work seven days a week, at least not when our children are young. We don't have husbands who are willing to stay home full-time while we climb the ladder of success; most of us probably don't even want them to. We are more likely to take the part-time option than our husbands, even knowing that its impact on our careers will be permanent and devastating. So are we simply getting what we deserve?

In a recent commencement speech at her alma mater, Barnard College, Joyce Purnick, the metropolitan editor of the *New York Times* ignited a firestorm when she said that she would probably never have made it to that position if she'd had children. All hell reportedly broke loose at the suggestion that the *New York Times* was not family-friendly to mothers; the fact that there aren't any mothers in senior editorial positions at the paper, and that the paper's most visible mother, writer Anna Quindlen, gave up her column to write novels and spend more time with her family, went unremarked.

I remember looking around the campaign plane during one presidential race and finding that almost every man on it was married, many of them fathers, while every woman was single. There was not a mother in the group. What mother would travel six days a week, for a year? Last time I checked, the senior White House staff is made up entirely of men with school-age children, and women without them. Lansing's proverbial two out of three.

The conservatives' response is that it isn't gender that blocks women's success but children, particularly in the early years. A study by the Pacific Research Institute, for example, found that among women and men ages twenty-seven to thirty-three who have never had children, women earn close to 98 percent of what men do. Overall, men with children earn the most, and women with children the least. Most working mothers accept not only less leisure time but lower wages in return for more flexible hours, a job location nearer to their homes or their children's schools and limits on last-minute out-of-town travel.

Having children early, as conservative Danielle Critten-don advises, may be biologically easier, but professionally far more difficult. Becoming a part-time manager is easier if you're already a manager. While what Stanford professor Vincent Fuchs terms the "economic disadvantage" for women with children is strongest between ages twenty-five and forty-five, "the effects remain throughout life." Of the 1.5 million white women in their thirties who earned over $25,000 in

1986, more than half were childless; only 24 percent of those earning less were childless.

In the conservative argument, children are seen as the answer to the claim of discrimination, rather than the form by which it is practiced. Marrying and having children increases a man's wages and decreases a woman's, but this is because of their different roles and responsibilities as parents, not because of discrimination.

The answer that liberal feminism has traditionally offered to the impact of children on women's success is to break the connection between gender and parenting. That's why *Weinberger v. Weisenfeld*—a case in which a father sought survivors' benefits under social security so that he could stay home and raise the children—is one of Justice Ginsburg's favorite cases, the one she continues to talk about, the one she brought up in a recent speech celebrating forty-five years of women at Harvard Law School. If more fathers would father more, not only could women mother less, but parenting would be valued more. A more equal division of household responsibilities, a more accepting attitude toward men who are househusbands, would liberate more women to compete and win in the public world. Freed of socially imposed gender expectations, there is no reason to assume that women would be less ambitious and more family-oriented than men.

Or so the liberal argument has traditionally been put. It puts women's choices in quotation marks, instead of changing the options. Meanwhile, the number of men staying home to raise children varies, depending on which figures you credit, between 2 and 5 percent. No revolution there. And while more men in dual-career marriages are taking on responsibilities like attending parent-teacher conferences, or taking children to scheduled appointments, a 1997 study at the University of Tulsa found that it is the scheduled appointments, if any, that fall to the fathers, while mothers are expected to respond to the unscheduled emergencies, which cause the greatest interruptions to work.

Most women who are the mothers of preschool-aged children, in fact, work full-time. Even among married mothers of preschool-aged children, 60 percent work, and of that 60 percent, 80 percent work full-time—double the figures of a decade ago. As Professor Ed McCaffrey has argued, the assumption that there is a vibrant part-time career track that mothers are affirmatively choosing is simply wrong, statistically speaking; most of those who do work part-time do so involuntarily, because those jobs, usually without benefits, are the ones that they can get. Liberal feminism is certainly right to point out that treating all women as mothers, and all mothers as less capable, is a self-fulfilling prophecy, the only result of which can be to exaggerate the impact of child-rearing on a woman's career. But waiting for the connection between gender and parenting to be broken is waiting for Godot; pretending that children have no impact on a woman's career is turning the exception into the rule. And what is worse, both the conservative and the liberal approaches blind us to the real discrimination that affects more women than any other form.

In *Griggs v. Duke Power Company*, decided shortly after the enactment of Title VII in 1964, the Equal Employment Opportunity Commission argued that the power company's requirement of a high school diploma for entry-level jobs amounted to race discrimination because it eliminated many more blacks than whites for consideration. The Court agreed, holding that, given the disparate racial impact of the diploma requirement, the company had the burden of proving that completing high school was necessary to performing an entry-level job. Height and weight requirements, common to many traditionally male jobs, were subject to similar scrut and almost uniformly thrown out.

Rereading *Griggs* two decades later is an eye-opening experience. It is a radical opinion, holding out the promise that Title VII would be a mechanism not only for eliminating explicit racial and gender lines, but also for changing the rules that govern the workplace. It defines the goal of antidiscrimination law as inclusion—not simply an end to intentional discrimination.

If the telephone company could be required to put more spikes in its poles so that those shorter than five foot seven inches could climb them, what else might employers be forced to do to redesign the workplace for female workers? Make room for mothers, perhaps. Some design issues are, admittedly, more complicated than others. Ordering up more spikes is easier than ordering corporate America to stop treating a period of part-time work as a permanent disqualification from the fast lane. But is it really so different, at least conceptually?

The idea that discrimination consists not simply of decisions made from a mean-spirited animus but also from the application of neutral rules and standards in a neutral way has been largely relegated to voting rights law. There are many he *Griggs* approach applied only to broad-

rt that generally govern at the entry level,

re subjective standards that tend to govern

-collar hiring, and hiring by small busi-

nesses. Where a woman claimed that she had been treated differently than a man—that she applied for a job, for instance,
for which she was qualified, but a man was hired instead—the
courts required only that the employer come forward and
articulate a nondiscriminatory reason for preferring the man;
unless the woman could then prove that the stated reason was
merely a pretext for discrimination, she lost. Employers have
become far more sophisticated in their personnel decisions,
while courts have become more wary of cases based purely on
statistics. The Supreme Court itself has pulled back from the
Griggs approach, and while Congress has reaffirmed the valid-
ity of *Griggs*, its potential to change the way we look at the
rules of work has never been fulfilled.

But the essential point that neutral rules don't necessarily
produce neutral results is still true. And its argument still holds
that when seemingly neutral factors limit a whole category of
people from participating fully in the workplace, those factors
deserve a form of strict scrutiny to determine whether they
really are necessary or just the way we've always done it—*we*

being the group that is advantaged by the status quo. The point is not to punish people—men—for their bad intent, for they may have had none, nor to turn women into victims without responsibility for their own choices, but to identify policies and practices that exclude half the population from achieving their full potential in the public world. Shouldn't we all be interested in knowing whether these policies and practices are really necessary? In short, the recognition that mothers earn less should be the beginning—not the end—of the inquiry.

Every year, after I teach *Reed v. Reed* in my gender discrimination class, we run through a list of hypothetical applications of the new, constitutionally mandated gender-neutral rule for picking the administrators of estates. In the first few hypotheticals, I have Ozzie and Harriet—the stay-at-home mom, the traditional family, and Ozzie always wins; I have a blue-collar woman, and a pink-collar woman, and a wife who works part-time, and they all lose too, at least if their husbands or brothers or whoever is contesting her appointment as administratrix has a better job. It is only when I get to Bill and Hillary, to the law-firm partner and the politician, to the extraordinary woman who has crossed into the public world, that the woman wins the contest.

What makes the man more qualified in each of these hypotheticals is his higher status in the public world of work. The fact that the woman might have known the deceased better, might know what he or she would have wanted, is almost always ignored. No student asks who handles the family budget, or who writes the checks. No one asks who the deceased was closer to. My male students almost always side with the man, but so do the women. We all think we are being objective, simply assessing qualifications. But the very question of what counts as a qualification, and how much it counts, is the loaded one that almost never gets asked.

Is it possible that much of corporate America does the same thing with mothers? It may be true that mothers work fewer hours than men while their children are young, but they also drink less, abuse drugs less, commit fewer crimes, live longer, have fewer heart attacks, get into fewer fights at work, are less driven to make costly business decisions for the sake of ego, are less likely to be sued for sexual harassment, or to quit for a better job. Whether women cost more than men, even under the most traditional analysis, depends on which costs you choose to consider.

Looking at children simply as a handicap to a parent's career ignores the fact that many of us get smarter when we become mothers, more mature, more responsible, more adept at handling people, all of which may make mothers more efficient, effective, mature workers. We'll take more shit. We'll swallow a lot to stay in the same place. We know how to manage hysterical babies without losing our cool. After having children, 52 percent of parents who are employed say parenthood made them more productive at work, based on a recent survey of more than one thousand adults for the Lutheran Brotherhood. Only 10 percent say they've become less productive.

Military men and women are valued when they make the move to the private sector, even though training for armed combat or nuclear war is not exactly useful in the private sector. Why is military experience, or government experience, considered more valuable than experience raising children, running a household, keeping the community afloat?

Judging qualifications, as my students do in *Reed v. Reed*, solely on the basis of public world accomplishments is neither neutral (it is certain to favor men) nor inevitable. It is not objective; it just seems that way because we've all been doing it that way for so long. If the problem is that we don't how to put a value on experience in the private world, shouldn't we figure it out? Or at the very least, let's examine how much we're holding it against women.

But women are disadvantaged not only because their advantages are undervalued in the assessment of qualifications (by judges who don't have them), but also because, according to the boys' rules they do play by, the qualifications that are among the most valued are ones where mothers are likely to be at the greatest disadvantage. Every workplace is different, and a few have instituted some changes. But as a general rule, the modern workplace, instead of becoming more flexible in terms of time as more women have entered it, is one where everyone is required to work more and where the penalty for dropping out may be getting more severe. The workday and the workweek are getting longer. Whatever motherhood means for an individual woman, what it means for everyone is lack of time.

If women had more political power in this country, or rather if they used the power they have, public policy would already be addressing this reality aggressively. Opening the schools earlier in the morning and keeping them open later in the day and during the summer makes so much sense in meeting the needs both of working parents and their families that economists express surprise that it isn't being done everywhere. As Harvard professor Claudia Goldin, an economic historian, pointed out, in response to a 1999 Council of Economic Advisers Report documenting the longer working hours of mothers, "the reason that the public schools don't open until 8 or 9, and close at 2 or 3, and stay shut during the summer is historical." Most of us do not have crops to be harvested or planted. We have children who need care, and mothers and fathers who are increasingly unavailable to provide it because of the demands of work. It is a problem that we have the power to solve, but don't.

But open schools, quality child care, and even the fat bank accounts of women at the top, who can afford to pay someone else to watch their children, don't respond to the desire to actually see our children and spend time with them. It is true, as *New York Times* reporter Susan Chira has eloquently argued in her book *A Mother's Place: Taking the Debate About Working Mothers Beyond Guilt and Blame,* that the children of working mothers do just as well on every measure as those of non-working mothers; what is most striking about Chira's book is that it still had to be written in 1998, that the issue has not yet been settled, notwithstanding the reality that a majority of mothers do work. But even if our children would turn out fine without us, even if their peers matter more than we do, most of us, for our sake if not theirs, do not want to miss the experience of watching them grow. Going days without seeing one's children, as many men actually do on the climb to the top, and in holding on once they get there, is viewed by most mothers as an unacceptable alternative.

"Sequencing," as it is often termed, refers to workers who alternate parenting and work. "The traditional managerial career path of a continued uninterrupted climb up the corporate ladder is still held in high regard," Rider University business school professor Joy Schneer points out. "If you violate that, there are repercussions." A 1995 study she conducted with Pace University professor emeritus Frieda Reitman quantifies that high regard. Schneer and Reitman compared 128 women who had never had a gap in their employment with 63 who had taken time off and then had gone back to work full-time by 1987. Even though the gaps involved were relatively brief—an average of 8.8 months—and even controlling for differences such as overall years of experience, the study found that even six years after returning to work full-time, women who took a break were still earning 17 percent less than those who hadn't.

And things may be getting worse since that study, not better. A decade ago, there were many who predicted that sequencing would be a growing phenomenon, with more and more employers offering workers the opportunity to leave for a year or more, and then come back to their jobs. But the trend, if you can call it that, seems to be headed in the other direction. In 1997, 2 percent of large employers offered leaves of a year or more; by 1999, it was down to 1 percent. Why? The conventional wisdom is that as the pace of change has accelerated, the ability to leave and come back has declined. New product life cycles have dropped by one-half or more since the 1980s to as short as six months, with companies constantly merging and restructuring. In her interviews, *Wall Street Journal* columnist Sue Shellenbarger found that mothers were leaving the workplace for shorter time periods, if at all, reflecting the consensus of management consultants, such as Ed Hersniak, that "the metronome is clicking about four times faster than it used to click. You can't truly focus on child rearing for 24 months and not get left in the dust."

Part-time work can also be a permanent disqualification from the fast track. A 1993 study of graduates of the University of Michigan Law School, which found a significant and growing earnings gap between men and women who started out with similar qualifications, identified a period of part-time work as the single largest factor explaining the gap, and found that its impact on salary continued to be significant years later, even after the woman returned to full-time work. Anecdotal evidence is overwhelming: dozens of women have told me their own stories, of how going part-time means leaving the fast lane with no prospect of returning.

Even women willing to put in the hours, even extraordinary women, find themselves confronting schedules that leave no room for children. One friend who is a comedy writer, at the top of a profession in which those over forty are a rarity and women's share of the jobs is actually declining, laments not how much she works but how the hours are perfectly structured for the lifestyles of men who take on no parental responsibilities. The workday starts at eleven o'clock, because these men like to sleep late and then work out. Lunch is from one to three, then they get going late in the afternoon, and work until it's time for their nine o'clock dinner reservations. They do that for four days, and on the fifth day, when they finish early, they all go out to celebrate and stay out really late.

My friend has a six-year-old, whom she would never see Monday through Friday if she followed their schedule. Literally never. Some of the guys who do it are indeed fathers; once or twice a week, they drag themselves out of bed early to slurp cereal with their kids, but other than that, they don't see their children Monday through Friday. My friend could afford to hire a nanny to take care of her child during the week and she has a husband who does more than most. It's not that she couldn't follow the guys' schedule, but that she won't. They put up with her leaving early (she also comes in early) and skipping the celebrations, and taking Halloween night off, because she's one of the senior writers in the room; she's been at it longer, with more successes under her belt than all but one or two of the men at the table. If she were a man, she'd be running her own show. But every time she takes off to do something with her son, one of the guys will say, "Well, if you have to." They make her pay, emotionally, every time she does it; she likes them less as a result. She is looking to leave. Their loss. But she is lucky. She'll find another job. Many mothers who earn far less than she does don't even have that option.

One way to look at the rapid pace of change, both in products and company structures, is to see it as a barrier to leaving the paid workforce for even a short period of time. No doubt, that is how most large corporations see it, in good faith. But there is an alternative view. The fast pace of change also means that everyone is constantly learning new skills; that last year's experience counts for less, not more, than it used to; that job shifting, reorganization, and new combinations are the norm and not the exception. Given that everyone is learning new things, working for new people, in new positions, why should missing a particular cycle count for everything? Why isn't working part-time a perfect solution, if you need one, to keeping up, if that really is the problem? Given that there is no stability in substance or personnel, why is a stable work record so critical? In the "old" days, when it was expected that employees would spend their careers with a single employer, I used to hear it said all the time that taking a break from work left women far behind precisely because the men had been there running things while they were gone. Now we're left behind because everyone is moving around. No matter what the scenario, women seem to lose. Could something be wrong with our calculations?

The idea here is that once you identify the rules, formal or informal, that disadvantage women far more than men, and mothers most of all, then you scrutinize them. In scrutinizing them, you commit to looking at them from both the conventional and the unconventional (some would say male-female) perspective. If they aren't really necessary, if you could accomplish your business some other way that doesn't exclude women, then you should. To continue running your business the old way, knowing that it disadvantages women unnecessarily, is discriminatory, or at least counterinclusive, which should be enough to convince, or shame, you into changing your ways.

If the lack of flexibility is holding back women, you ask, how much would greater flexibility cost? Why must people make partners in their twenties and thirties, rather than in their forties? Why must the years be consecutive? Why can't line experience come later? Why can't you do it on a conference call? How much travel could be eliminated? How else could it be handled? What about allowing people to team up, the way real estate brokers do, and divide a partnership or position, or hold it jointly? Why can't women double up, cover for each other to give them control over time, the way doctors do?

Many have held out hope that technology would bring limitless flexibility to the workplace, allowing us to choose our hours, work from home, negotiate in pajamas. Whether it could or not is debated, but for many working women, what advanced technology means is more work, not more flexibility.

The managing partner of a branch office of a big law

firm, one of the few women to climb so high, scoffs at all the usual excuses for why it is that the practice of law cannot be more flexible in ways that would allow women to succeed who are willing to work hard but need flexibility. It doesn't matter where you are, she argues; the good and bad news is that you can work from anywhere, have instant access to all the resources that you used to have to go the library to examine; and communicate instantly with people around the world. You can have a meeting in your pajamas in front of your computer after you get the kids off to school. You can do legal research at 1 A.M. Much of what we used to travel to do can now be done without ever seeing the other person. Documents can be exchanged instantly. Show me a law firm office run by a woman, and I'll show you an office with more women, more diversity, and more flexibility, at no cost in profits.

But that's hardly a pattern you find across the board. Studies to date suggest that while many more people are working out of home offices connected to the world by computer, most of those who are connected to their employers that way are still required to put in long hours in person, with technology making it easier to connect to work in your home time, not vice versa. The first shift is getting longer, and what sociologist Arlie Hochschild brilliantly termed the "second shift" now has two masters.

The traditional answer as to why work rules don't need to be scrutinized this way is because the market does it for you. If employers are behaving foolishly in ways that cost them money, somebody will come along, figure that out, and do it the better way. If mothers, or women for that matter, are worth more than the market thinks, then someone should come along and make money on the insight. Worth is measured by markets; competition corrects mistakes, assuming all the actors are rational.

Of course, there is a market response at work, both in the flight of women to small businesses, which offer greater flexibility (and are more likely to be run by women), and in the creation of "mommy track" jobs, which individual women feel grateful to have. There is a strong case to be made that the fact that there are more second-tier choices for mothers than there used to be undercuts rather than furthers change: Why make a mother a partner, if she'll settle for "senior counsel"? If she'll say thank you to any promotion, you don't need to give her the better one.

Talk to individual women and they will tell you that they feel they have no choice but to accept what is offered, even if

it involves making less money and forsaking future opportunities. Expectations and ambition are shaped by the organizations within the market, and not simply brought to the market
by individual actors. Women may settle for too little, precisely
because the market has encouraged them to do so. We act
singly, when our greatest power would come from collective
action. We act based on the assumptions of what is realistic,
not what is right. Does this mean that women are somehow
less than rational actors? Not necessarily. But it undercuts the
claimed neutrality, much less inevitability, of what the market
produces, and raises the specter that the market responses are
undercutting the push for change, not feeding it.

Even the most conservative economists recognize that
while providing a more generous leave policy or greater flexibility might make sense for the economy as a whole, there
may be disincentives for a particular employer to be the first
to offer such benefits, particularly if what they are focused on
is an (exaggerated) estimate of its short-term cost. As Professor
Lawrence Katz of Harvard explains, the fear that a generous
leave policy might attract employees with no long-term interest in the company means that "even employers who want to
provide generous benefits will not do so." Now, I might argue

that women who are offered a generous leave policy are likely to be very grateful, and that women in general may be too loyal to their employers, and demand too little in return, but Katz's calculation comes closer, no doubt, to the way employers see it.

That is because the market is not a gender-neutral institution, nor is it one in which men and women, or whites and minorities, wield equal power. The market did not solve the problem of race discrimination, even where it was clearly irrational in economic terms; it took the courts to do it.

With rare exceptions, the standards that measure success in the public world continue to be standards applied by men to men and women. The men who are the decision-makers bring to the task of valuation a set of stereotypes and assumptions about women, and so do the women to whom they are applied. Even my smartest female law students take a while to see the game in my *Reed v. Reed* hypotheticals, to start asking questions about what counts as a qualification—or a disqualification—and why. And that is in a class on gender discrimination, not in a corporate office.

The number of corporate cultures, outside the world of small business, that are defined by a woman or women on top is as few as the number that see mothering as valuable experience. That is the ultimate significance of all the Catalyst studies, whatever the cause. The number that see the promotion of women as a measure of their own success is only slightly larger. The result is that certain questions are never even asked, certain assumptions never validated, and certain stereotypes become self-fulfilling prophecies.

The corporation, John McGinnis writes in his *Wall Street Journal* review of Lionel Tiger's book, *The Decline of Males,* may be the last refuge of Man as Hunter, the one place "where men can still flourish by using their ancestral skills," and where "controlled aggression" is actually rewarded. Many high-placed women agree.

How we judge people is inevitably a measure of how we evaluate our own success, and apply it to others. That doesn't feel like discrimination. It feels like fairness when you're doing it equally across the board, when you are applying to others the same tests you apply to yourself.

In constitutional law, this is known as a "we-they" problem. When "we" make rules that disadvantage people just like us, then courts need not provide more than minimal scrutiny to the results. But when "we" make rules that disadvantage "them"—particularly if they are a discrete and insular minority, which women are in the upper echelons of corporate America—then strict scrutiny of the rules is required. In the law, strict scrutiny is generally fatal in fact. In corporate America, the rules and standards, the measures of qualifications, and the assumptions about costs that disadvantage women are almost never put to the test.

What would happen if they were? The Family and Medical Leave Act of 1993 is an instructive case in point. For years, business blocked the passage of legislation requiring larger employers to grant unpaid leave to workers who needed it to deal with medical and family emergencies, including childbirth. When the legislation was finally passed in 1991, it was vetoed by President Bush, at the urging of every business association and trade group. The assumption, throughout the years of debate, was that the act's primary beneficiaries would be pregnant women, and that it would impose a huge burden on business.

Those assumptions proved to be wrong. The bill was one of the first to be signed by President Clinton after his election in 1992. Now, years later, even its staunchest opponents concede that their predictions were unduly dire. In fact, more than 90 percent of the businesses surveyed say their experience under the act has been favorable. As many men as women have taken leave to deal with crises in their families. Maternity is not the only game in town; that turns out to be one of those *Frontiero v. Richardson*–like assumptions that isn't even true, much less being true of everyone. Indeed, the experience has been so favorable that extensions of the act have been proposed, to allow shorter leaves for school meetings, parent conferences, and the like, and there is broad support for the effort.

Expanding the Family Leave Act is only one of a number of legislative steps that have been proposed to deal with the family-work conflict. There is another proposal on the table to allow states to use federal unemployment compensation funds to cover family and medical leaves, and even legislation to add parents to the list of those who cannot be discriminated against in employment under Title VII.

But new-fashioned discrimination presents challenges that are not easily met by traditional legislative approaches. Proposals for extending family leave to doctors' appointments and PTA meetings, and even the prospect of limited compensation for what would otherwise be unpaid leave, only go so far. Women, and men, who take leave may have legal protection, but whether they will be promoted or disfavored, advanced or permanently held back, remains a decision that no one from the outside is scrutinizing. Preventing discrimination against parents is staunchly opposed by the business community, which claims it will give rise to too many meritless claims. And even if such a proposal could be enacted, it probably means less than appears at first glance: It would only bar employment practices that disadvantage those whose responsibilities as parents have no impact on their work, not force a reevaluation of how costly those impacts really are. What is most striking about the proposal is not its boldness, but the fact that there are currently still employers who will explicitly not consider a person for a job if they are a parent, regardless of whether parenting affects their work.

That is why you find mothers, as I did, leaving the graduation brunch, who literally lie to make their children invisible. It is why many women understand that their years as a parent will count for less than nothing—will count against them in corporate America—when they return to the workplace. If you don't fight 'em, you have no real choice but to join 'em, which is why motherhood is still destiny.

SIX

The Comfort Factor

The picture that has come to define President Clinton's friendship with his closest adviser and counsel, Vernon Jordan, is the picture of the two of them sitting together in a golf cart. What better symbol of the comfort level between the two, and therefore of Jordan's power as the president's best friend, than that? The file photo of Hollywood mogul David Geffen, used to demonstrate his close connection to President Clinton, is also a golf shot, although Geffen is otherwise not particularly known as a golfer.

When Catalyst researchers asked senior corporate officers

what they thought was holding women back, the most often cited answer by the male officers was that it was a pipeline problem: just a matter of waiting for women in the pipeline. The response of the female officers was notably different. The most often cited answer offered by corporate women was the "comfort factor": that is, the comfort of the men at the top with having women in their midst, or at least the particular ones who make it through the door. Similarly, when asked what they considered essential to success, the female executives cited "developing a style with which male managers are comfortable" second only to exceeding performance expectations.

Carole Goldberg, the former president of the Stop & Shop grocery chain and a director of Gillette, teaches seminars to women about how to make it in corporate America. Her advice: Play golf. "I'd suggest women who want to build their visibility and networking skills to know the role golf plays in it." "She's a golfer," I say to a powerful male friend, describing L. D. Acheson, corporate lawyer, justice department official, and Hillary pal. "A golfer," my friend says, "now that's interesting." Hazel O'Leary, the energy company executive who became secretary of energy, has said that she learned to play golf to advance her career, and thought it was a valuable tool. Researchers have studied corporate women according to whether they play golf, and the golfers appear to be more successful.

"How many of you play golf?" I asked an audience of 1,700 women at a YWCA lunch one day. Precious few hands went up. More men than women play golf. According to recent figures, roughly 40 percent of the new golfers in America are women, a record high, but many of them are nonworking women, with more leisure time than the average working woman, not to mention the average working mother. Who has time to learn to play golf, women ask in frustration, much less get good enough at it that men who have been playing for decades will want to play with you? Maybe we can encourage our daughters to learn this sport when they are young, but is the older generation doomed?

In a world in which more men than women play golf, in which golf clubs have traditionally discriminated against women and working women in particular by not admitting them altogether except as wives, and by reserving the best tee times for men, a strong case can be made that doing business on the golf course is sex discrimination. Does the president discriminate in his choice of friends? By the *Griggs* standard, almost certainly. But what do you do about it? Sue him? Or find some other way to make him comfortable?

Developing a style that men are comfortable with does not mean dressing, acting, or behaving just like a man. Ann Hopkins discovered that the hard way when she came up for partnership at Price Waterhouse. In a strikingly candid evaluation, Hopkins was told that while she had brought in business for the firm, her style weighed against her. She was too aggressive, particularly for a woman; she was advised to be more feminine, get new clothes, get a haircut. She brought suit claiming sex discrimination.

Hopkins won. The Supreme Court held that the comments about her femininity could amount to gender discrimination, at least theoretically. But the Court also held that a plaintiff claiming such discrimination would not be entitled to a partnership if there were some other non-discriminatory reason justifying the firm's decision not to promote her.

The problem is that in a professional context, where decisions are subjective to begin with, there is almost always some non-discriminatory reason that can be cited to a court. Remember the Philadelphia attorney, Nancy Ezold, who ultimately lost a sexual discrimination case on appeal, when her employer successfully claimed she did not make partner in her law firm because of her "lack of analytical ability." No one is perfect; once employers learn that a certain kind of frankness counts as discrimination, they won't be so frank, which is altogether different from actually changing the standards. The advice Ann Hopkins was given is precisely the sort of advice women give one another these days.

"The ideal woman," one senior man tells me, "is married, but has no children; attractive, without being too sexy; strong, but not too tough; ambitious, but not too aggressive. More buttoned up than Ally McBeal, less sweet than Mary Richards, fewer edges than Murphy Brown; a good athlete, and a good sport; active in professional groups, not women's groups; not a feminist, but . . ." I send a student out to research the ideal corporate woman, and she comes back with a prototype who is thin and smokes cigars. I'm not sure about the cigars, but there are no fat women in any of the up-and-comer lists.

No fat men either, to be sure. Not every man is good in sports. The comfort factor also excludes men who are not macho enough, or too religious, or too family-oriented; the only thing worse than a woman who is too devoted to her children is a man who wants paternity leave and doesn't like sports. Men who are too much like stereotypical women don't make it. Still, most corporate women believe that men are allowed a broader range within which to fit than women, and that the range is more familiar to them and comes to them more easily, not only because issues of sexuality and attraction are generally excluded, but also because the character, traits, and attitudes that we think of as coming most naturally to men are those that are valued most at work. Typical men succeed; typical women do not.

The comfort factor refers not only to how you look, but how you lead. Studies have found that when women use the same direct management styles as men, they tend to be rated roughly equally. But other studies find that many women don't use that style: They talk less, and let others talk more; listen more, exercising influence and wielding power indirectly. There are countless examples of men reacting negatively to such styles of leadership. Why are you asking us, a woman university president recalls men saying to her in early meetings, faced with a management style that was radically different from her predecessor's. Aren't you the president? She was, and still is. Mary Jo White, a United States attorney, describes how different the dynamic is in a room when a woman—or at least a woman like her—is running the meeting; how the discussion is more open; and conflicting views are more often and more readily voiced. Women talk more, and men talk less; a striking reminder of the advantage that men enjoy most of the rest of the time.

A strong case can be made that corporate America could do with more of a consensus style of management, and that female managers have something valuable to teach their male colleagues. Harvard professor Rosabeth Moss Kanter has been making that case persuasively for decades, as has University of California professor Judith Roesnner. But women whose leadership style varies from the male norm run the risk of being seen as tentative, indecisive, and worst of all, weak—and such judgments can be the kiss of death when they are made not by those who are working for you, but by those for whom you work. It is one thing for a university president to laugh in retrospect; or a United States attorney to celebrate the differences, and quite another for women on their way up to expect the workplace to adapt to them.

Indeed, the subject of management styles raises precisely the sort of tensions between reinforcing traditional, and sometimes inaccurate, stereotypes about women—the very stereotypes that have been used to hold women back—on the one hand, and embracing the male model and denying to women who differ from it, particularly in the most traditional ways, a fair chance of success.

Consider, for example, the results of a Catalyst study 1986 report summarizing existing research and concluding that executive women are more like executive men in terms of their behavior, goals, personalities, and motives than they are different from them. Those results were reaffirmed by the findings of Ann Morrison, Randall White, and Ellen Van Veslor, who reviewed test scores for thousands of managers compiled by the Center for Creative Leadership, and found that on most of the stereotypical dimensions, executive women did *not* differ from executive men: They were not less dominant in leadership situations, not less self-confident or secure, not better able to reduce interpersonal friction, not more understanding or humane. One of the few significant differences they did note was that executive men feel more in tune with their surroundings, and are more likely to feel equal to the demands for time and energy encountered in their daily lives.

But these studies raise as many questions as they answer. Do women as a group really approach the business of management precisely the same way men in general do? Or is it that in a world in which selection, promotion, and mentoring decisions are made almost exclusively by men, in which the male approach is the management norm, do women succeed by acting like men, whatever their own instincts? Are the successful women the ones who are most like the men, or the ones most capable of acting like them?

To get a job as a law professor, candidates must give a presentation before the faculty about the scholarly work they are doing, which is then subject to extensive discussion and dissection in faculty meetings. Sitting in those meetings at Harvard throughout the 1980s, I became aware that there were certain words that tended to be used, disparagingly, to critique the presentations of women. *They were tentative, not ambitious enough, not far enough advanced; they didn't break enough new ground, their work was too limited in its scope.* The men, on the other hand, would be given credit for boldness, ambition, setting out to do something important; taking on the big names; pushing the envelope; embarking on a major effort. The irony was that the substance of the presentations did not break down so neatly along gender lines: In fact, the women were often more ambitious than the men, taking on bigger issues, trying to do harder things than fit together a dozen cases or apply well-established economic principles to new areas of the law.

What was going on? It wasn't what they were doing, but

what they said they were doing. Women would come in and apologize before they began; downplay their goals; admit to the limits of their accomplishments. It wasn't that they were less ambitious, or not as smart and capable; they were just less arrogant. But it didn't matter. We women on the faculty started to hold coaching sessions in advance for women applicants, in which our major advice was usually to recast their description of their efforts in more grandiose language.

The researchers at the Center for Creative Leadership, while taking the position that the research establishes few behavioral or personality differences between executive women and executive men, acknowledge that women executives are in fact perceived to be different by what they call the "savvy insiders" who can make or break their careers. Because women are perceived to be less effective than men in management situations, they must prove they are more effective— they must be seen as better than other women, as exceptions to the rule, without forfeiting their femininity in the process. The success stories were not women who proved that the stereotypes were wrong, but only that they did not apply to them. The more manly a man is in corporate America, the better. The same is not true for women. Whatever the real differences between men and women as managers, the perception that women are weaker managers creates a reality in which they must be even stronger; the comfort zone for women requires that they disprove differences and counter expectations that may or may not be real in the first instance, without straying too far and becoming too "masculine" in the process.

Social science literature sheds further light on the inconsistent demands placed on corporate women. While the subject of sex differences is a loaded question in legal and political circles, it has been the subject of somewhat more dispassionate study by psychologists and behavioral scientists. In 1974, Eleanor Emmons Maccoby and Carol Nagy Jacklin completed an in-depth review of more than 1,400 published studies on sex differences, and their conclusions provide the benchmark for subsequent analysis of the issue. What was perhaps most significant about their findings, particularly given the times, was the number of perceived sex differences, which were in fact *not* established by the studies. Maccoby and Jacklin concluded that, contrary to popular belief, girls possessed just as high a level of achievement motivation as boys, were similar in their persistence on tasks, and equally influenced by the reactions of others. Tests of general intelligence were similar, although there were some differences with respect to specific abilities; girls did not in fact seek more security than boys and were no more responsive to social approval and reinforcement. One of the few areas where clear sex differences did emerge was on the subject of aggressiveness, where a number of studies confirmed that from about the age of two, boys exhibited a higher level of verbal and physical aggression.

Thousands of studies since 1974 have tested Maccoby's and Jacklin's findings of the existence of very limited differences between the sexes. There has been substantial evidence that a sex difference in mathematical ability, which Maccoby and Jacklin placed at adolescence, begins before that, as does a sex difference on visual spatial ability. However, both abilities are recognized to be amenable to training. The sex difference in verbal ability has been found to be even weaker than Maccoby and Jacklin had surmised from their findings. As for aggression, further study has found that men and women are in fact equally likely to respond with aggression when provoked, but men are more likely to initiate the aggressive conduct.

Other sex differences to emerge since the 1974 study, Gary Powell argues in his book *Men and Women in Management,* may turn out to owe more to the status differences between men and women than their biological differences. Thus, the finding that men tend to be more influential and women more easily influenced in most settings—certain to be invoked by some to prove that men are stronger managers—may prove no more than that men tend to be more powerful—more capable, that is, of exercising influence, and therefore do so more often. The typical status difference between men and women, with men in the higher level position and women in the lower level position, gives them the authority to exercise influence. Similar status differences may explain the findings that women have higher nonverbal communication skills than men; those with less power have more reason to communicate indirectly, and greater need to interpret the nonverbal cues that reflect the judgments of others.

These examples suggest just how slippery the lines are between sex differences, considered to be biological, and gender differences, which are the product of socially constructed roles and expectations. If women use indirect influence more often than men, as some researchers suggest, is it because they are born that way, brought up that way, find themselves in subordinate positions where that is the only way to exercise influence, or are they simply perceived to be acting indirectly whatever they do?

Consider for instance the findings of researcher Kay Deaux, who found that men and women tended to explain their own success differently: Men were more likely to attribute their success to skill, and women to luck. In practice, this is a distinction that works to the absolute disadvantage of women. As one law firm partner explained to me, when a man has a particularly good year, everyone expects that it will be the first of many, proof that he has the skill it takes to get business; when a woman has a particularly good year, everyone's first reaction is to assume that it is an exceptional year for her, the product of good fortune and not special skills, with no expectation that it will necessarily be repeated. Compensation tends to follow these expectations, as do better assignments, appointment to the management committee, and adoption by mentors, making it more likely that the differential expectations will become self-fulfilling prophecies.

As it turns out, Deaux found, it is the difference in expectations that produces the difference in explanations. Deaux concluded upon further study that men and women in fact use the same processes to explain success; the difference was initial expectation for performance; women credited luck for making up the difference between the expectation that they would perform less well than men and the reality of doing equally as well. Expectations for performance gave rise to sex differences, not the other way around.

Whatever the "real" sex differences, expectations plainly do vary. The study of gender differences, the differences in expectations of what is "masculine" and what is "feminine" reveal a far broader array of differences than the study of discernible sex differences. Inge Broverman and her colleagues concluded, in 1972, based on a study of college students, that men are perceived as being more competent than women but less warm and expressive, and being competent is a more valued trait than being warm and expressive. Challenging the neat division between what is "masculine" and "feminine," posited as opposite ends of a single scale, researchers in the mid-1970s introduced the concept of androgyny to include highly valued examples of both male and female behavior, the person who was both competent and warm, both forceful and expressive, the new ideal. Sandra Bem developed a scale in which masculinity and femininity were defined as independent sets of characteristics, rather than as opposing tendencies, with the individual who possessed the best of both—high self-esteem combined with a flexible response mechanism including both masculine and feminine behavior—considered to be the androgynous ideal.

But not so fast. Bem's work was criticized for being value-laden, and more tellingly, for failing to recognize that the desirable characteristics of a woman were not perceived, by either men or women, to be of equal value to the desirable characteristics of a man. Masculine characteristics were considered more desirable—men could succeed by simply being masculine, while women could not succeed by simply being feminine. Indeed, later research suggested that masculinity produces more positive outcomes for individuals in American society than androgyny, which means that even the woman who manages to combine the best of both sets of expectations will still be at a disadvantage as compared to the man who simply meets expectations.

And therein lies the rub for the female manager seeking to get ahead by developing a style of being and leading with which male managers are comfortable. The way Ann Morrison and her colleagues describe it, the challenge for women is to find the acceptable band that represents the overlapping portions of two hoops, the masculine and the feminine: For women to succeed, "it was essential that they contradict the stereotypes that their male executives and coworkers had about women—they had to be seen as different, 'better than women' as a group. But they couldn't go too far, to forfeit all traces of femininity, because that would make then too alien to their superiors and colleagues. In essence, their mission was to do what wasn't expected of them, while doing enough of what was expected of them as women to gain acceptance." Morrison calls it a narrow band, but it might just as well be considered a vise.

In seeking to make men comfortable, women end up tightening that vise. As noted earlier, when asked what is necessary for women to succeed in corporate America, women executives placed developing a style that male managers were comfortable with second only to exceeding expectations in their ratings. But on closer examination, the two go hand in hand. The essence of "comfort" lies in a woman's ability to defy expectations, even as the factors that make that so difficult are themselves the product of the differing expectations of men and women. Women make men comfortable by proving that they are not like other women, thereby affirming the very stereotypes of women that become, for most, self-fulfilling prophecies. Because it is expected that women will do less well, they must do better.

Consider again the women who came to Harvard interviewing for jobs and sounded insecure, tentative, less sure of themselves. Is that because as women, we are naturally more modest and self-effacing than men? Or is it because of the expectations, shaped by history, that both men and women bring to this particular table? The men on the faculty come to the presentations by a female candidate knowing that women don't often make it at Harvard as professors; the women come knowing that women tend to get chewed up and spit out by an institution waiting, half expecting, that they will fail. So they sound tentative, do they? You'd be crazy to sound otherwise.

It is a natural human tendency—except when it comes to sex—to gravitate to those who are most like you, to be most comfortable with those you can relate to, those with whom you share the most in common. Take away sex, which most smart and ambitious men and women mostly do at work, and men are most comfortable with men, women most comfortable with women. Take away men, advocates of single-sex education (myself included) argue, and you will see women at their best, their most ambitious, speaking out, running everything. Put the men back in the room, and all of a sudden, they are the ones who are editing the yearbook, running the student government, dominating the board. What makes the men most comfortable is women who don't challenge them, not women who do; women who aren't like them, not women who are. This is not true of every man, to be sure, but the number of men who duplicate themselves over and over

again in one corporation after another, the number who sur-
round themselves with male confidants and then react with
anger at the very idea that they have excluded women, suggests that it is true of many of them.

So does the experience of one woman I met who was a
scratch golfer, a woman with no handicap, a better player than
all but a few of the men in her work circle. "Does it help you
at work?" I ask her. She laughs. "You think they like me better because I can beat them?" she asks. "No way. Besides, it's
not really about golf. It's about riding around and talking
dirty and being guys. I spoil it for them when I come."

So what is a woman to do? Go to the spa? If men bond in
the golf cart, why not have women's day at the spa? Last year,
a major bank sponsored a one-day power confab for executive
women that featured an afternoon of spa activities, including
massages, facials, and hairdressing. A Denver law firm sponsored a similar affair the year before. Notably, these events
tend to merit news stories, which is itself a measure of how
unusual they are; golf games don't merit much news coverage,
unless the President of the United States comes along. But the
reality is that there is far more power on the golf course than
there is at the spa. In a world in which men constitute 98 percent of the senior managers and 99 percent of the CEOs and

inside directors, more can be accomplished in the men's room than in the women's room, and pretending that spa days can balance golf games gives women short shrift. Besides, many women balancing jobs and family have no time for spas; my girlfriends laugh when someone says we should all find time to go to the spa together. Fantasyland. Instead of Little League? Networking among women, valuable though it is, is no substitute for including women in informal gatherings with the men, particularly ones that take place during the work week, and not in "free time" that we don't have.

The bottom line on the comfort factor seems fairly straightforward: Squeezing into the vise will only get you so far. And so long as it is a vise, many women will lose out in the competition. Discrimination? Sure. It's golf. How do you make golf count for less? Or better yet, how do you change the game to one women can play?

SEVEN

Changing the Face of
Corporate America

To look at the number of women who have made it to the top of corporate America, you might think that it was virtually impossible to recreate the workplace in ways that would make it more likely for women to succeed. Three Fortune 500 CEOs, 1.1 percent of inside directors, less than 3 percent of top management, persistent pay gaps, declining partnership promotion rates, and a generation of less ambitious women have all been enough to convince many people that being no worse than everyone else is good enough. I hear this every day from women and men when I query them about where their firms and companies stand in terms of the advancement of women. As one lawyer explained to me, a partner and a woman no less, "We've lost two women partners in the last two years, but we're still no worse than the competition." MIT was no worse than Harvard. Harvard is no worse than any other institution. We have redefined failure as equality.

But there is not an industry or a profession in which there are not some exceptions to these general rules. In banking, there was Bank of America, which stood out prior to the merger with Nations Bank in 1998 because of the number of highly placed women and is again reclaiming a place on the best employers list. In high technology, there is Lucent Technologies, where Carly Fiorina earned her stripes, working for a CEO determined to be inclusive. In food services, there is Kraft and Sara Lee; in cosmetics there is Avon; in higher education, there are the women's colleges. There are law and accounting firms where the rates of promotion are declining, and half the women leave in five years. But there are others who find themselves promoting more and more female partners every year, and hiring associates in equal numbers.

At Proskauer Rose LLP, a New York–based law firm, the senior women decided that they would make the promotion of women through the associate years a priority for the firm. They have mentoring circles that review promotions, provide advice, and focus on results. Helping the younger women brings the older women together, giving them more power within the firm. As a result of their work, Proskauer is known as a woman-friendly and family-friendly firm, which enhances their appeal among both men and women at recruitment time.

The accounting firm of Deloitte & Touche instituted a program aimed at retaining and promoting women as a "business imperative for the 1990s," and partnership promotion rates increased from 8 percent in 1991 to 20 percent in 1997; as of 1998, 11 percent of Deloitte & Touche's partners were women, the highest level in the "Big 5."

Morrison & Foerster, an international law firm, offers a flextime policy for both partners and associates who must care for children or adult relatives, and a three-month paid maternity leave followed by an optional three-month unpaid leave. The firm also pays 95 percent of any fees for backup childcare. Many large law firms have no female litigation partners; at Morrison & Foerster, however, the litigation department in Los Angeles is headed by a woman who was named a partner while on maternity leave. "Unheard of," says a friend who gave up on being a partner at a large Los Angeles firm when she had her second child.

The Lincoln National Corporation, based in Fort Wayne, Indiana, established a women-at-work task force to examine recruitment and leave policies in the early 1990s; the task force has evolved into the Women Executives Group, which continues to monitor the participation of women. As of 1998, Lincoln had two women on its board of directors, and women comprised more than 28 percent of its executives at the corporate vice president level or above, and 21 percent of its managers.

Catalyst gives awards every year to companies that are taking innovative steps to recruit and retain women; *Working Woman* publishes lists of companies that are women-friendly. What is striking about all the different lists is that the companies cited have almost nothing in common: They are of every size and type, located in every part of the country, in every sort of business, manufacturing as well as service.

What puts them on the lists is not structural but personal. It's a human decision, not a company characteristic. In every case, the effort to be better than everyone else, instead of no worse, begins with one person, or more than one person, deciding that it will be done. How do companies change? Very simply. People with power use that power to demand better; they insist on results, and they get them.

For many people, "affirmative action" has come to mean that unqualified people should get the job or the contract or the place in the class over those who are more qualified solely on the basis of skin color or sex. I oppose that form of "affirmative action," and so do most people, unless it is adopted to remedy past discrimination, or in a situation where there is a compelling need for diversity. The Supreme Court has declared absolute preferences unconstitutional when practiced by public entities in all but the narrowest circumstances.

But the original conception of affirmative action was very different. It was based on the recognition that, left to their own devices, most institutions would not change; they would continue to hire and do business and promote the same people they always had, consciously and unconsciously ignoring those who had been intentionally excluded in the past. The purpose of establishing goals and requiring an explanation when the goals weren't met was to hold people's feet to the fire and force them to take a second look. It's not about hiring or promoting unqualified people but about ensuring that the most qualified person, and not always the most familiar one, gets the nod.

This is the way it works in the military. If an officer continually promotes whites over blacks, he has to explain why, to justify to his superiors why his numbers are off. And miracle of miracles, the military is the one place in America where it is routine for whites to work under blacks.

We need to count. Corporate America is expected to produce profits, required to report each quarter, forced to explain any downfalls, and judged by its results. Why not do that with respect to the inclusion of women, particularly at the top? A workplace without women should be suspect and scrutinized accordingly. It's not a quota, any more than profit projections are. But the determination both to count and to demand accountability reflects a judgment that success is both possible and important; you're expected to succeed, not just try hard. If you fail, you have to explain why, and it better be good.

Losing half the potential pool of candidates, or almost that, for any position or job is foolish, particularly if it can be avoided. You get a better army with women in it, because you can set standards higher; a larger pool of applicants means greater competition and higher selectivity. That's even more true in a world of high training costs and shortages in key labor markets, where technology sets high standards. If we all weren't so used to seeing women leave the workforce and seeing sex-segregated workplaces, we'd realize how high a price we're paying for their departure.

If you think of the lack of retention and promotion of women not as a moral question but as a problem that's limiting the talent pool and needs to be solved, it can be. The kinds of obstacles that women confront as women—the unspoken assumption that you aren't as good; the demands and desires of motherhood; the adaption to a male comfort zone—are by no means insuperable. The critical point is to see the absence of significant numbers of women in positions of power as a problem. Once you do, it can be approached the same way businesses address other problems. You get all the facts, analyze what's causing the problem, and set about to fix it.

If motherhood is a major obstacle, as it is almost everywhere, then flextime, job sharing, backup childcare, and telecommuting options can be afforded. If senior men inevitably choose younger versions of themselves to mentor, as they often do, then formal mentoring programs that offer women equal access to mentors can be instituted. If informal networking on the golf course and the ski slopes excludes women from valuable interaction, then other forms of formal and informal networking, such as family retreats, need to be planned, and senior managers need to be made aware of the fact that many women enjoy watching sporting events as much as men. If there's reason to suspect that unspoken assumptions about women's abilities and ambition may be leading to less desirable assignments and fewer opportunities, as they did at MIT, then these suspicions need to be examined by task forces of senior men and women, or by the management committee, or even the board, to assure that hiring and promotion decisions are made deliberately instead of unconsciously.

In short, the pipeline needs to be examined from beginning to end to see how it works differently for women, and should not be assumed to be fair because it is neutral. Women, as women, need a way out of the work chase when they are raising their children, but they also need a way back in when their family circumstances change. Children grow up. Their mothers often need to return to work to pay for their education. The worst horror stories I hear these days are from women trying to reenter the workplace after raising their children, only to confront both sex and age discrimination. The young men who interview them need to be held accountable for their unspoken discomfort about supervising their friends' mothers and for their assumptions that an older woman will be less productive than a younger person.

Obviously, approaches need to be adjusted to the particular population and environment. Things can be done well, or not so well; corporate culture has to support the changes. There are expert consultants who can be brought in from the outside to come up with recommendations for action, just as they do when companies are trying to increase their profits, or stem their losses. What's holding progress back is not that change is impossible but that most companies still aren't trying, or do it so half-heartedly that they might as well not do it at all.

The fact that conscious discrimination has given way to unconscious discrimination not only leaves women feeling confused, it leaves men feeling guilt-free. If the men on top don't think they're discriminating—and most of them don't; they'll tell you that they'd like nothing better than a qualified woman for a top job—what's the reason to change? Who needs a task force if we're good guys? Here and there you'll find an enlightened boss who understands the economic benefits of inclusion, but the majority of CEOs have "bigger" things to deal with, where there is real pressure. If no one is demanding results on where the company stands with respect to women, it just doesn't make the list.

My guess is that there are very few institutions in America that could withstand the scrutiny that MIT applied to itself. Or rather, they would emerge just as MIT did. They would find that at the entry level, women and men started out roughly in the same place, but that younger female employees confront challenges of balancing home and work, family and job, that the men don't. They would find that as they climb up whatever ladder there is, women often have to fight for what is automatically given to men; that assumptions about their ambition, determination, and commitment, or resentment of their success, leads them to come out short on significant fronts. They would find women who don't make it because they're too masculine, and women who don't make it because they're too sexy. They would find that critical contacts and discussions take place on golf courses, at sporting events, etc. Forced to confront all this in the light of day, they would see these things as problems and vow to fix them. If they see what they're doing, fewer will do it. Creating a task force with high enough ranking men to convince the rest is half the battle because so few workplaces (particularly ones without existing task forces or committed bosses) will survive the examination. Asking the questions will produce the agenda. Feminism in action.

The question, then, is: How do you make it happen? How do you shine the spotlight where it needs to be? It takes power to do that, and the willingness to use that power.

One woman may not be able to make it happen, unless she's the CEO, or his wife, or a particularly determined director. But three women can. Maybe even two. Twenty years has made a difference. Women have not made it to the top, have not changed all the rules, but every company has three women who have made it far enough that together they have power they aren't using. Three female partners, three tenured women, three female directors or trustees or senior officers— one you can ignore, but three today could be more tomorrow, and even if it's only three, they'll get attention. Stories of sex discrimination in big companies are, in media terms, sexy. If three senior women in any company in America ever walked together because they'd hit the concrete ceiling, it would hurt. If two female directors insisted on a task force to examine issues of promotion and retention, who could say no?

It is acceptable to practice discrimination, but not to preach it. You become the villain. Once exposed, it can be deadly. Particularly if it's a company that depends on women as purchasers, as most do.

Very few successful women in any occupation have ever had the experience of being promoted because they are women. If you listen to some of the conservative talk shows, you'd think it's happening everywhere, but speaking for myself, I've never seen it, and most women I know have never sensed that they were ever preferred that way. It's the opposite you hear over and over, the stories of women who had to do more, prove more, than the men. This understandably leaves them with a strong sense of having made it on their own. But that's not entirely true. It was not many years ago that no matter how good a woman was, she would not be given the necessary opportunities to prove it. The climate has changed; indeed, as Hewlett Packard's hiring of Carly Fiorina proved, promoting a woman to a high-visibility position can get you enormous positive publicity, which is why it is so striking how few companies take advantage of the opportunity.

This is particularly true in the case of women who serve on corporate boards. They are not just like men. According to the studies cited by Zweigenhaft and Domhoff in their examination of the new power elite, fewer of the female than male directors had attained leadership roles in corporations before being invited to board membership; women are more likely than men to come from non–Fortune 500 companies, to be consultants rather than executives, academics or even volunteers, an unheard-of description of any male director. They may well bring better judgment to the boards than the men, but there would have been no occasion for that to be demonstrated without the women's movement and Catalyst in particular.

Ten years ago, there were only a handful of women on corporate boards. Today, only 1.1 percent of the inside directors are women, but more than 10 percent of the outside directors are. The reason this has changed is not because corporate America suddenly woke up one day and realized that there was something wrong with having meetings attended soley by men; they still have those. The major reason things have changed is because Catalyst started counting the number of women on boards and making a fuss about the results, and all of a sudden, miracle of miracles, the numbers started growing. Indeed, there has been a direct correlation between the calls that go out when Catalyst begins its annual census and the ability to find qualified women to serve on corporate boards. The humming fax machine, as Catalyst president Sheila Wellington describes it, is playing the tune of power.

In its 1999 census, Catalyst, for the first time, extended its count to the companies in the bottom half of the Fortune 1000. Those who think that inclusion is only a problem in the biggest firms should find the results surprising and troubling. Nearly 40 percent had no women at all; another 40 percent had only one; and only 20 percent had more than one. Now that Catalyst has started counting, the numbers should increase.

There is an important lesson in the Catalyst experience for the women who make it onto the boards, Fortune 1000 or otherwise. There are women today who are in positions to exercise power who don't understand why they are there. It is not that they are unqualified to serve on the boards, or to hold their offices, but that being qualified would not be enough. They are also there because they are women, and that should impose on them an obligation to use their power on behalf of women.

There was only one woman on the tenured faculty at Harvard Law School when I was a student. Notwithstanding her outstanding reputation in her field, she had labored for some sixteen years as a "research associate" before she was promoted to tenure. Her promotion, not coincidentally, came at a time when the federal government was doing its own count of the number of women on the Harvard faculty. Harvard's first response to the count was to reclassify all of its librarians as tenured professors—albeit ones who were paid less, had fewer rights, and had no role in governance. When that didn't satisfy the government, which had given Harvard a great deal of money (the carrot aspect of its insistence on nondiscrimination), they actually found a few women to make real professors.

One of the women they found didn't teach any first-year classes, or even any of the basic second- and third-year courses, meaning that most of us never would have had a chance to meet her, let alone take a course from her. So we decided to make an appointment to see her instead, our little group of activists, the women's support group that met weekly at the bar where I worked. We told her our concern: that we would go through three years of law school without a single female professor, and that not only would we suffer for that, but so would the men in our classes, who would never have the experience of seeing a woman with that kind of authority and power. What, we asked, can be done to get more women on the Harvard Law School faculty? Why were there so few? This was her answer: The reason that there are so few women on the Harvard Law School faculty is because there are none who are qualified. It was precisely the same answer that the most conservative, tradition-bound men gave us at that time.

None of us dared to contradict her. But she was wrong; in her case, doubly so. Like the men, she accepted as neutral criteria credentials that almost no women had, like presidency of the law review or a Supreme Court clerkship, credentials which, as I was to discover, were harder for women to achieve than for men. The irony was that she didn't have them either. Even more important, she had no sense of the special responsibility she bore precisely because she was a woman. She was qualified to be a professor—we didn't doubt that, even if her own standards called it into question—but she had been promoted because she was a woman. Had the Department of Health, Education, and Welfare not been looking over Harvard's shoulder, she would still be a research associate. She owed her job, her title, and her position to the accomplishments of the women's movement and the pressure it had generated, and yet she felt no obligation because of it. She may not have signed up with the women's team, but the team had taken her on and promoted her, and now she was turning her back. It's worse than being ungrateful, closer to treacherous than just bad manners.

To say that a woman is there *as* a woman is in some respects unfair. Men aren't required to represent men. But that's because men, as men, are fully represented, while women are not.

When I ask women who have "made it" why they don't demand more women on their own level, or take the agenda of women in the company as theirs, or seek out women vendors, or raise a stink when the headhunters return with the usual male suspects, the answer I often get is that if they do, the men will think less of them. It's like teaching sex discrimination. The men will think that they are "one of those" women, not the kind of woman they like; the fear is that their stature in the men's eyes, what they consider the source of their power and success, will decrease. In a corporate culture in which women must prove how different they are from other women in order to succeed, championing a woman's agenda can appear to be a career-ender. And I suspect that there are still some, even unconsciously, who think they have more power as the only woman in the room.

It's not so. With few exceptions, rooms with one woman in them are rooms run by men, in which the woman will never be on top. It's significant that 70 percent of the Fortune 1000 boards of directors have no more than one woman sitting on them. Getting more women to the table almost always builds the power of women in general, and the ones who got them there in particular. Consider what happens on a board. The more board women there are, the more power the men will see the women as having, particularly if they sense that the women consult with each other on key issues. An individual woman, thinking only of herself, might consider this demeaning; why think of me as one of the girls, instead of as one of the boys? But it is also an opportunity. By consulting one another, women increase their individual power; a bloc of four can be significant, and anyone who can influence it (especially the senior two, who were responsible for bringing on the other two) is especially powerful, certainly more powerful than she was when the only vote she controlled was her own (and that was probably controlled, at least in the eyes of the men counting, by the man who claims he got her on the board).

Get new women promoted and your power grows. They're indebted to you, and they owe you. You're viewed as a kingmaker. Colleagues realize you must be taken seriously. Power begets power. If those on top see you differently, they also see a woman who understands how to use power and build it; "one of them," perhaps, but one to be dealt with respectfully, and carefully, which certainly beats being taken for granted.

Those who work in blue-collar jobs are more accustomed to thinking about their interests in collective terms; only by acting collectively can they hope to negotiate successfully with management. Among professionals, the individualist streak runs strong; the essence of the antidiscriminatio

ciple is the right to be judged as an individual and not ac

ing to one's group membership. But if gender enters into

evaluation, as we know it does, it doesn't disappear by ignor-

ing it, but by recognizing the reality and acting collectively to

respond to it.

"Ask for everything," advises Harriet Rubin, the author
of *The Princessa: Machiavelli for Women*. We are half the population, half the vote; we control half the wealth and more than
half the purchases, but women rarely ask for half of anything.
Rubin's point is that by stepping back and actually asking for
something colossal, you can change the rules of the game. By
asserting power, you get more power; muscles get stronger by
flexing them. Machiavelli was in it for himself, but he didn't
start off disadvantaged because of gender.

One friend who serves on a corporate board tells me how
difficult it is. She is one of the few board members who has
never run a large company. That, she says, not her sex, is what
limits her influence. Unfortunately, they go hand in hand, and
so long as they do, it's the job of boardwomen to groom their
replacements, to see that there are more women who have run
something in the next round.

Mary is a lawyer in a firm with more than five hundred

lawyers. She is a high-powered partner who does transactions, works crazy hours, and has to travel. She has two kids under seven; she keeps a lot of balls in the air. One of the younger female associates came into her office recently and said to her, "I don't want your life." Mary didn't fight with her. There are days she doesn't want it either. The only thing worse would be not having it. She thrives on the challenge, most of the time. Meanwhile, she has enough clout in the firm that she was able to block the plan to eliminate part-time attorneys, after a study had found that the profit margin was smaller than for full-time lawyers. It wasn't that they were unprofitable, mind you; just *less* profitable. The fact that they were all mothers was something that no one had pointed out until Mary did. "Who could make that kind of a recommendation?" I asked her. "What was he thinking?" *"She,"* Mary corrected. It was a woman, with no children, who wasn't thinking.

The most important step to getting more women in very high places is just to get more women in the room. When there's only one, the chance that all the women will fail is too high, and the burden on the one who's trying can be insurmountable. I remember when Harvard Law School used to bring in one woman at a time as an assistant professor, and the whole school would follow her struggle. Meanwhile, there might be two or three new white guys with glasses, at least one of whom might have a very rocky time. But which one? Who knew? They got to fail and then succeed, and still people wouldn't be sure which of the guys with dark hair and glasses it was. And even if they were sure, there was no lesson in it for anyone else, one way or the other.

It isn't only the women at the top who have power, collectively. Women in the middle can help women at the bottom; women at the bottom can help women get in. It used to be commonplace for women in any workplace to get together separately from the men to compare notes and give support. That tradition gave way as things "improved," or at least when we started acting as if they had. Not enough.

If a major employer doesn't give decent maternity leave, ten pregnant women marching in front of headquarters with strollers and signs can put that issue on the table. Every city could have its own mini-Catalyst that issues reports on where women stand in major local corporations. Women on the outside can count, even if there are no women on the inside to insist on it. Which bank has the most women? Which insurance agency? Which department store chain is run by women, and which has no women on top? Which drug store chain refuses to stock emergency contraceptives for women because they think doing so would be bad for business?

How much money do you spend every day? Would you be willing to buy a different brand of sandwich bread, or a different kind of laundry detergent, or fly a different airline to reward companies that promote women? The sandwich breads taste the same, and the detergents work the same; but if the companies are different in ways that reflect our values and priorities, why shouldn't we shop accordingly? Many of us would, or at least we would be willing to, if we knew, and remembered.

Information can be power if we use it. Technology makes it easier than ever to do politics. Women as consumers have so much potential influence that even the prospect that we would take action is enough to begin the process of change. United Airlines finally added a woman to its board in 1999, after making Catalyst's lists year after year, and after a number of writers, myself included, started mentioning it prominently on every occasion, along with some suggestions. Hazel O'Leary, the former secretary of energy—and golfer—was elected to the United Airlines board in 1999; she was available for some years before that. But my first choice was always Oprah. Can a strong woman make a difference? Yes.

And sometimes, you just have to sue. The law is still the most powerful wedge for opening doors that remain closed even to the most extraordinary women. Sometimes there's no substitute for a lawsuit to get the attention of the men on top, and to change the system as a whole. It's a bit like a judicially enforced task force, with a much higher price tag.

Allison Schieffelin is a principal in the institutional equities division of Morgan Stanley Dean Witter & Co., which is as firm an establishment as you can get. After being passed over for managing director and seeing men she believed to be less qualified promoted over her, and never getting invited to play golf with clients, even though she's a golfer, Ms. Schieffelin filed a complaint with the Equal Employment Opportunity Commission (EEOC), alleging sex discrimination in violation of Title VII. Morgan Stanley denied everything and refused to hand over documents. The EEOC took Morgan to court, insisting on records of any American employee who had ever complained of sex discrimination. The EEOC won in court. After reportedly taking evidence from other women who had worked in the department, the EEOC ruled in June 2000 that it was persuaded that Morgan Stanley engaged in a pattern and practice of discrimination against Schieffelin and other "similarly situated women." The "similarly situated" language is most important: It means that the case can be pursued as a class action, with the possibility not only of damages for every woman affected, but also a remedy that requires structural change and even sets goals for the promotion of women.

In July 1998, Smith Barney agreed to spend $15 million on efforts to hire and promote women over a four-year period, in addition to paying damages to individual women who were subject to discrimination. The settlement came in a lawsuit that began with allegations about the "boom-boom room" in the basement of a New York branch office, and broadened into claims of companywide discrimination. Merrill Lynch was sued, at almost the same time, by a woman who claimed that women were discriminated against in the manner that leads and referrals, walk-in accounts, and the accounts of departing brokers were distributed. Smith Barney ended up with 1,950 individual claims of discrimination to settle, while Merrill had 900. Mary Stowell, a partner in Stowell & Friedman, who represented female plaintiffs against both Smith

Barney and Merrill, told the *Wall Street Journal,* "A number of companies have re-examined their employment practices, taking a look at their population of women and aggressively trying to get women into higher paying jobs where there can be room for them. I think this turmoil of the last four years has been very healthy turmoil."

Allison Schieffelin isn't allowed to talk about her complaint. She's been passed over two more times since she filed it. The EEOC also upheld her claim that Morgan Stanley had retaliated against her since she filed the complaint, no longer sending her to recruit on campus and not allowing her to mentor younger employees. It can't be easy for her to go to work every day, particularly now that her complaint has hit all the papers, with some reports suggesting that Morgan Stanley could face as much as $100 million in damages. But if Schieffelin was right that sex discrimination was blocking her career, she wasn't going to get ahead by being a good girl. And thanks to her, things are almost certain to be better for the women who come up next. They'll owe her. We all owe somebody. The way you pay back is by helping the next wave.

EIGHT

Sexual Power

He is an extremely powerful man.

She is a young staff aide.

She didn't want to bring it up. She would have gone to the grave with the story.

He says it never happened.

His supporters say she had a crush on him.

He says she is being used for political purposes.

She gets pilloried.

He says he is being attacked by opponents who resent his power.

His supporters see a vast, extremist conspiracy.

He wins. He is one of the most powerful men in the world, even though her account is the one most people believe.

It's Anita Hill and Clarence Thomas. It's Monica Lewinsky and Bill Clinton. It's a feminist nightmare.

There's a line of argument that goes: nothing is better for feminism than to be forced to define the rules when it is our friends and not our foes who have been accused of wrongdoing. I've made the argument myself. If it's not good enough for our sons and brothers and husbands, it's not good enough for someone else's.

All true. But if you asked me whether I'd rather spend two years of my life educating people about what's wrong with sex between a powerful male boss and an intern or what's right about it, there's no doubt where I'd come down.

So what was I doing defending the most inappropriate consensual relationship that a law school professor could dream up? How could I have supported Anita Hill and then not stand with Paula Jones or Monica Lewinsky or Kathleen Willey? How could I question Clarence Thomas's fitness to serve on the Supreme Court, and then turn around and defend the president against those who were seeking to remove him from office? There are three answers to that question. The first two are easy. The third is what makes sexuality in the workplace such a double-edged sword for women.

The first answer is personal: I believe in loyalty. This does not mean standing by people only when they are right. That isn't about loyalty; that's just good judgment and common sense. Loyalty is about standing by people when they're in trouble, when they need you, because they need you. In 1988, when I was running Michael Dukakis's presidential campaign, during the endless fall when I was getting battered for decisions I couldn't control, when Democratic politicians were ready to head for the hills, afraid of getting caught in a landslide, Bill Clinton called me every day to find out what he could do to help.

The second answer is political. I know politics when I see it. I was doing the same thing defending Bill Clinton as the Rutherford Institute was doing representing Paula Jones in their first-ever foray into the area of sex discrimination. I was doing the same thing all the anti-Clinton conservatives who had fought against the laws prohibiting sexual harassment were doing, the same thing Bob Packwood defenders were doing, the same thing most people in Washington do every day. I was doing politics. It happened to be allegations of sexual harassment that were the ammunition this time. But the fact that everyone was on their usual political sides is as good proof as you'll find that the core of the dispute is not about what's welcome and what's unwelcome in terms of sexual harassment law, but whose ox is being gored.

Those are the first two reasons, which are more than enough to get me in the chair with a microphone clipped to my jacket and an earplug and an audio check. I don't always say everything I think on television, but I do adhere to my principles, both in the positions I take and in how I express them. I tell the truth, even if it's not the whole truth. Which means that I had to find a way to reconcile Anita Hill and Monica Lewinsky as a matter of principle, even if the motivation for the debate was political. I had to convince myself that there was a real difference, that I was not sacrificing the cause of sexual abuse for a veto on partial birth abortion.

I was certainly not alone in this struggle. Many women who had supported the president found themselves deeply conflicted about his relationship with Monica Lewinsky and his efforts to hide it from Paula Jones's attorneys. For me, that conflict was particularly intense, not only because I count the president as a friend and an ally, but also because I have spent much of my professional life fighting to reform the law regarding rape and protect women against sexual harassment. Putting the law on the side of women has been my way of fighting back, resisting to the utmost, which is what used to be required of rape victims, albeit after the fact.

I was raped twenty-five years ago, on the eve of my graduation from Wellesley College. Having finished classes a semester early to save money, I was living in a small apartment in Boston's Back Bay, on Commonwealth Avenue. Like everyone else in the Back Bay, my parking place was in the alley behind my building; the alleys ran between the main thoroughfares, and the parking lots branched off of them. My parking space cost almost as much as my apartment. I had already been through one job as the office manager of a vending company (where I was paid less than the man who swept the floors in the storeroom, because he had a family to support). I moved on to a job as a cocktail waitress in green pants and a white halter top, balancing a tray full of drinks and dancing with dollar bills threaded through my middle finger, for ninety-nine cents an hour plus tips. The job was within walking distance of my apartment; I would walk home at 2 A.M., barefoot because my feet hurt so badly. I was fired for trying to organize the waitresses so that we would each make more money working fewer nights. By the time I was officially graduating college, I had found the job that would help me pay my way through law school: I was a bartender at Mahoney's 499 Lounge in Somerville, a working-class bar where my boss was the owner's daughter, and you could wear whatever you wanted. I worked nights; I would drive home late, park in the back, and walk through the alley. I was careful, but I wasn't afraid. Back Bay was one of the safest neighborhoods in Boston.

Fortunately, I wasn't raped walking home alone at 2 A.M. from my previous job in the green pants and halter top. And I wasn't raped running out of an alley onto the better-lit street at 1 A.M. after driving home from my job as a bartender. I'm grateful for that, because I have no doubt that I would have blamed myself if I had been, not to mention the lectures I would have heard about women being out alone at night. I was raped in broad daylight, at 5 P.M. on a Thursday evening, wearing a long sleeve blue shirt and blue culottes, nothing sexy at all, having stopped at the supermarket on the way home from graduation rehearsal. I had pulled into a space in the little parking lot off the alley, pushed open the driver's side door, grabbed my two bundles and my purse, and was about to step out when a man with an ice pick told me to push over, shut up, or he would kill me.

Later, I jumped out of the car as he was backing it out of the space; the only good thing about those car-crammed little alley parking lots was that it took a lot of concentration to get out of a space, which gave me my chance to escape. Two women from a neighboring building saw me standing there crying. I went up to their apartment, and we called the police.

Compared to what happened to other women in those days, I had a relatively easy time dealing with the system—but mostly for the wrong reasons. The first question the Boston police officers asked me was whether the man who raped me was "a crow." "A crow?" I asked. This was Boston in 1974, the year they integrated the schools. A crow was a black man. The man who raped me was black.

The history of rape is a history of racism as well as sexism, and the interplay of those concepts is as clear a guide to the allocation of power in America as any. Until the death penalty was ruled to be cruel and unusual punishment when applied to the crime of rape, black men could be executed in this country for the crime of rape, and regularly were. But it was the race of the victim that determined the likelihood of conviction, as well as execution: Rape of a black woman was considered to be noncriminal behavior in circumstances that would have justified the imposition of the death penalty were the victim white.

"Did you know him?" the police officers who picked me up asked. I was taken aback. Did I know the man who had put an ice pick to my throat and threatened to kill me? No. I didn't know him. Would it have mattered if I had?

In the months and years that followed, as I found the courage to talk about being raped, I discovered just how much it mattered. "Did you know him?" people would ask. And when I said I didn't, the sympathy level went straight up. "Oh, so you were really raped," they would say. As opposed to what? As opposed to not really being raped?

To be raped by a black stranger in the city of Boston in 1974 was to be "really raped," a legitimate victim. Those two answers put the police on my side. Oh, I had to tell the story over and over again, to one group of male officers after another, back in the days when police departments had yet to have special units for rape, or female officers assigned to do interviews. But no one questioned my version or my motives. Perhaps because of that, they went out of their way to warn me. "Are you sure you want to go forward with this?" one of the officers asked me kindly. "You know what defense lawyers do to rape victims," he explained. "Anything you wouldn't want to have to answer questions about?"

"Not in Back Bay," the doctor who examined me at Boston City Hospital said. "I can't believe this could happen in broad daylight between Commonwealth and Newbury." What was he suggesting? That it didn't happen? That I'd made it up? And on and on he went, as he gave me the shot for penicillin, took swabs, commented on the safety of different Boston neighborhoods. Too much later, a woman pulled the curtain aside and introduced herself as a representative of the newly formed Boston Rape Crisis team. She apologized for being late; neither the police nor the emergency room staff had called at the first report of a rape, as they were supposed to, as they usually do today. Would I like her to be present for the rest of the doctor's examination, she asked. Yes. She told the doctor to shut up about what he could and couldn't believe, and he did.

They never found the man who raped me. I started law school in the fall.

Two hundred years ago, Lord Chief Justice Matthew Hale said that rape was a crime easily charged but hard to prove, and harder still to disprove, even by an innocent man. I was horrified when I came to understand, first as a student and later as a professor, how much the usual principles of the law had been twisted to accommodate stubborn views of the dangers of vindictive and spiteful women wrongly accusing a man of rape. Even in the 1980s, courts continued to apply different rules in rape cases than in all other crimes, making it both more difficult and more painful to pursue a legitimate complaint.

Some of these rules were procedural. Victims of rape might be required to report promptly or lose their right to complain, while for other crimes, it was enough that the statute of limitations had not expired. Some jurisdictions required that a rape victim's testimony be independently corroborated or the case would be dismissed, instead of leaving it to the jury to decide, the way it's done for other crimes. Others insisted that a cautionary instruction based on Sir Matthew Hale's approach be given to jurors, reminding them that rape is a crime easily charged, and hard to disprove. There were also evidentiary rules, making the victim's sexual past fair game, while the defendant's was considered off-limits. And there were substantive rules: force or threat of force were narrowly defined, to the point that some courts would not consider the defendant's past history of violence, as the law does in self-defense cases.

Two imperatives fueled the rules. The first was Hale's: the concern that women would simply lie, creating incidents that didn't exist, turning consensual sex into allegations of rape to get even. Making rape difficult to prove, and scrutinizing the victim's past and her motives, were intended to protect wrongly accused men from conviction. The second imperative was to make sure that the line between sex and rape was drawn so as to protect men who are forceful in their desire for consensual sex from being accused of rape. The law did this by enforcing definitions of force and resistance that ignored the realities of physical size and strength, allowing a man to use physical strength to overpower a woman, and requiring the woman to do more than say no to demonstrate her nonconsent.

The rules were not applied uniformly. In cases where a woman claimed she had been raped by a stranger, particularly an armed stranger, the strict rules were rarely applied. Resistance was excused; corroboration unnecessary or invented; sexual history irrelevant. It was in cases that might have been consensual in other circumstances, cases involving men and women who knew each other, dated, worked together or went to school together, that the rules were most forcefully applied, making it both painful and difficult for the woman to pursue her complaint.

By the 1980s, it was hard to argue out loud that women claiming rape were presumptive liars who could not be smoked out by the usual rules of the criminal law. In fact, the studies suggested just the opposite: that rape was underreported, particularly when committed by someone known to the victim.

Instead, the prevailing argument was that in close cases, it was entirely possible that both the man and the woman were telling the truth; that she was telling the truth when she claimed that she said no and felt forced, and that he was telling the truth when he said that he reasonably believed that she was consenting to sex. It was not that the woman was lying, but that two different versions of reality could coexist, and that in those circumstances, the man's version had to be the one that the law credited, since the law requires *mens rea,* or bad intent, as an element of the crime.

What made this a modern, liberal argument was that unlike the traditional, Matthew Hale approach, it did not presume that the woman's account was inherently suspect. But it also did not require the man to respect the woman's definition of her sexual autonomy at the expense of his own. Instead, holding that both accounts might be "true" and that therefore the woman might feel that she had been raped, but the man was not a rapist, privileged a man's right to have sex when he wanted it, using force as she would define it, denying women the power to exercise autonomy by saying no. She might say no and mean no, but he didn't have to believe it. The law would protect her sexual autonomy not as she defined it, but as he perceived it; what was reasonable was what he thought, not what she did.

In the law, reasonableness marks the line between sex and rape, between private and public, between what is your business and what is ours. On one side of that line, the individual, in this example the man, is free to pursue his sexual satisfaction, to act autonomously regardless of the consequences to others. On the other side, society intervenes through the law to limit his autonomy in order to protect others from injury. One side of the line is private; the other is public. The question is where to draw the line.

Law reformers, myself included, argued that evidence of a woman's past history of consensual sex was largely irrelevant and highly prejudicial when the issue was whether a man used force to have sex. We argued that the focus should be on what the man had done wrong and not what the woman had, that verbal nonconsent (saying no) should be enough to convey nonconsent, and that force or threat of force should not be limited to guns or knives or extrinsic violence. We argued that men were being given too much freedom, and women too little protection. We were trying to move the line between what is of public and what is of private concern.

It is a measure of the political power of women in the last twenty years that we won that fight in the courts and legislatures. Every state reformed its rape laws, eliminating the resistance requirement, creating degrees of rape, and getting rid of the spousal exclusion. As a matter of law, no means no. Shield laws were passed protecting women from unnecessary intrusions into their private lives. Federal law went a step further, providing that evidence of the defendant's sexual past was admissible, while evidence of the woman's was not.

The effort to protect a woman's right to say no extended from physical force to economic coercion. If your boss tells you he won't promote you unless you pay him off, that's blackmail. But telling you he won't promote you unless you sleep with him used to be considered seduction. Why, feminists asked, should physical force be the only form of coercion from which women were protected? Why should women be subject to sexual abuse because they can't afford to quit their jobs? Telling a woman she will lose her job if she says no to sex carries as much force as holding her down. But the law doesn't prohibit coercion used to secure sex in the same way that it does coercive efforts to secure money. What the law does prohibit is sex discrimination at work.

Beginning with Professor Catherine MacKinnon's book *Sexual Harassment of Working Women,* feminist reformers argued that conditioning the benefits of employment on a woman's response to unwelcome sexual advances was itself a form of sex discrimination. Essentially the argument was that a similarly situated male would not be subject to such pressure; he had the opportunity to be hired and fired for a better reason, or at least another one. The fact that all women weren't being treated this way did not negate a finding of sex discrimination; it was a classic case of sex-plus discrimination, like pregnancy or being the mother of a small child. The courts agreed. The workplace changed.

But cases remain difficult to prove, and painful to endure. On the criminal side, prosecution and conviction rates have not increased substantially. On the civil side, federal law notwithstanding, women who complain of sexual harassment often find themselves treated the same way that rape victims traditionally have been. The "nuts and sluts defense," I'd been calling it for years, never expecting that I'd be called upon to employ it.

Matt Drudge is a friend of mine. He has made some very serious mistakes. But after hearing him speak at USC, and pulling all the clips, I was struck by the fact that this young Internet journalist was being castigated by the traditional press corps without any acknowledgment that they do the same things every day. Matt had been telling everyone that the White House was after him, because he was being sued by Sidney Blumenthal, whose job was to feed tidbits to the press corps. I wrote a column saying that the press corps was a bunch of hypocrites for pretending they had nothing in common with Drudge, and then–press secretary Joe Lockhardt (at Blumenthal's urging) called the editorial page editor at *USA Today* and complained about it. Joe later apologized; he happens to be a terrific guy. But Matt couldn't have been more thrilled. The White House must really be after him to go after me. I was his proof.

Which is why I was among the first to know about Monica Lewinsky. Matt e-mailed me to tell me what was happening at *Newsweek* magazine, where the Monica story was being killed. The president and an intern. A Beverly Hills babe. "What are you going to do now?" he asked.

I was at a cocktail party the next night. The story still hadn't broke. "I wish I needed something from the president," I said to the new Los Angeles chief of police, Bernard Parks. "Before this is over, he's going to owe me." He looked at me like I was crazy. Now he thinks I'm smart.

I never believed the president's public denials. Of course he would lie about sex with an intern. Who wouldn't? As for the question of whether he'd do it, I thought he would. He has a weakness for women who offer themselves up to him, which happens all the time. He's charming, he flirts, he loves women, and there are still millions of women in this country who would have happily traded places with Monica Lewinsky. Every woman who spends five minutes with him believes he has eyes for her, which he does, during those five minutes. I shake my head at these earnest young men in the Administration who claim that their hearts were broken when the president lied to them. What did they expect him to say? They knew him. They knew his weakness. Why would they even ask?

The president never lied to me, but, then again, I never asked. When we talked about Monica Lewinsky, we assumed *arguendo* (lawyer-talk for assuming for the sake of argument) that he had an inappropriate sexual relationship with her, and we took it from there.

But I never believed Paula Jones, who claimed that the president exposed himself to her and then used his power to limit her career because she turned him down. And I never believed Juanita Broaddrick, who claimed that the president had raped her two decades before. I didn't assume anything *arguendo* in talking to him about those cases.

He might say yes to an intern in thong underwear, but he would not abuse women sexually. Sexual harassment law is not aimed at those who are sexual but at those who abuse their power to violate the sexual autonomy of another person. Bill Clinton doesn't need to do that, and he wouldn't anyway. He was my friend, and I believed that he was being wrongly accused. And the rules I had supported and helped to create, rules which create a one-way ratchet in the plaintiff's favor when it comes to digging dirt in rape and sexual harassment cases, and limit the defenses available to the defendant, were the means of waging that attack.

Jonathan Stockhammer was a sophomore at Brandeis when he was convicted of raping a woman who had been his best friend. As it happened, she was bigger than him, continued to be friends with him, invited him to her home even—factors that might have weighed in his favor. His case came up for trial the same week as a major television movie on date rape, and fearing the reaction and the forces of political correctness, he opted for a judge trial. The judge convicted him.

On appeal, Stockhammer hired Nancy Gertner to represent him. Nancy is an old friend of mine, and now a federal district judge, recommended for the bench by Senator Ted Kennedy. She was one of Boston's most prominent feminist attorneys at the time Stockhammer hired her. Her argument on appeal was not that no means yes; on appeal, you're stuck with the facts as found below. Besides, it was the 1990s by then. Instead, Nancy argued that Stockhammer's lawyers were entitled to access to the woman's psychiatric and counseling records from the hospitals and counselors; that the fact that the judge had examined some (but not all) of these records *in camera* (that is, by himself in chambers) was not enough to afford the defendant an adequate right to defend himself. The defendant and his lawyers needed to see them for themselves. Stockhammer was on the verge of going to jail, his life in ruins, based on the testimony of a deeply troubled woman, and he had a right to establish just how troubled she was.

The victim in the Stockhammer case did all the wrong things that I have argued for decades aren't "wrong" in the sense that they prove much about the truth of the charge. Yes, she waited a long time, but so did Anita Hill. The fresh-complaint rule has been eliminated because judges and legislators have finally come to understand that the shame of being raped and the perceived hostility of the system provide ample explanation for why a woman would wait. Yes, they knew each other, were best friends even, and might have been drinking, but betrayal by a friend can be even more serious than the injuries inflicted by a violent stranger. That's always been my argument. Yes, she got counseling, and may well have said things in those sessions that she would never want repeated. But didn't I?

Nancy Gertner was convinced that Jonathan Stockhammer was innocent, and that his conviction was a product of the politicization of rape and the forces of political correctness. A student of mine, a woman who was herself the mother of a college-aged daughter, read the transcript of the trial and was equally convinced of his innocence. Jonathan Stockhammer, she told me, was a naive, slight, sexually inexperienced young man, not a rapist. The woman was a confused, troubled, insecure girl, afraid of her father, distraught over losing her boyfriend, the very woman Matthew Hale warned us about. "She was nuts," my student, a feminist, said to me.

Maybe. Maybe not. Maybe he made her nuts. Confused, troubled, insecure, and frightened girls are easy targets, which makes them the most likely victims of both rape and sexual harassment. A male judge believed her, but the Massachusetts Supreme Judicial Court reversed the conviction, holding that the defense had a right to the records of her counseling and treatment after the rape. Nancy won. The feminist community in Boston felt betrayed. The rape treatment centers announced that they would henceforth stop taking notes. *Stockhammer* was subsequently moderated to have the judge inspect the documents privately first to determine their relevancy, but the promise of privacy has been compromised, and the fight continues in the Massachusetts courts, with the rape crisis centers losing in the most recent rounds.

Women who bring high-profile charges, claiming either rape or sexual harassment, invariably find their reputations attacked, targets of a public "nuts and sluts" defense. Remember what happened to Patricia Bowman in the William Kennedy Smith case? Character assassination. But even low-profile cases have their risks. Any defendant who can afford an investigator will hire one. Former enemies come out of the woodwork, and some people will always think of you as a troublemaker who ruined a poor man's career over nothing. No matter how good your record, I tell young women, you need to understand that in that situation, you are vulnerable.

Consider what the army's highest-ranking woman went through, as a result of her complaint that the man named to oversee complaints of sexual harassment in the Army in fact made unwelcome advances to her during an October 1996 meeting. Lieutenant General Claudia J. Kennedy did not complain promptly about Major General Larry Smith's alleged groping. She did not race to her superiors and demand action, file formal or informal charges, tell all of her colleagues what had happened. Had she done those things, people would credit her account more. But she didn't. She took it like a man (exactly the wrong way to take it), kept it to herself, no doubt knowing that her own career would be jeopardized as well if she pursued a complaint.

General Kennedy did not come forward until, with her retirement looming, she saw a man she remembered harassing her named to the army's top post overseeing complaints of sexual harassment. When she did, she was called a liar because of inconsistencies in statements about where and when she complained, and was investigated criminally on the basis of "pretty thin" (the army's description) allegations of misconduct in the mid-1980s received from a retired officer. Complainer beware. Don't sue until you've decided to leave. If the highest-ranking woman in the Army, the poster girl for all women in the military, is vulnerable if she steps forward, imagine what could be done to the rest of us?

If Nancy Gertner was right about Jonathan Stockhammer's innocence, what else could she do? Unwanted sexual advances rarely occur with witnesses present. Assume, if only for the sake of argument, that he or someone in his position is actually innocent. Assume that the president didn't expose himself to Paula Jones, as she claimed; if he had, he would have settled the case on whatever terms were available, and avoided everything that came afterward. Lawyers joke about how hard it is to represent an innocent client, but it's true. They don't want to settle, but in cases like this, proving your innocence is not easy. How does he prove that he didn't do something that happened behind closed doors years ago? The most he can hope to do is cast enough doubt on the woman's account and the woman herself to save his career from being completely ruined, or prevent himself from going to prison. Imagine if it were your husband or brother; imagine if it were your son; imagine if it were you. Would you want to know if the woman making the accusation had been hospitalized for mental illness? Would you want to know if she was receiving counseling, now or then? Is there anything you wouldn't want to know about her?

President Clinton signed the bill protecting victims of rape and sexual harassment from courtroom inquiries into their past, but that didn't stop his lawyers from investigating Paula Jones, right down to men she had allegedly met in bars, which is precisely what Republicans did to Anita Hill. When it got out, feminists who had been holding their tongues stood up to protest. Politically, it was a mistake for the president to offend his allies. But as a lawyer, William Bennett was doing his job.

I have seen many honest victims raked over the coals when they complain and have counseled many more who had good reason to fear what would happen to them if they complained. I have seen and heard of many men who get away with tormenting one woman after another, knowing none will complain.

The law is based on the assumption that we should be erring on the side of the plaintiff and not the defendant, a presumption with greater claim in the civil than criminal context. A defendant in a criminal proceeding has a constitutional right to raise a defense. It's easy to argue that privacy should be respected when the issue is whether a woman consented to sex with an ice pick–wielding stranger, or even a date who beat her up, but as we move the line from violent to forced sex, the swearing contest becomes all the more critical. Hale was always wrong about rape being a charge easily made; it isn't. But our success has made it hard to prove, as it should be, but also harder to disprove. Even if you eliminate all vestiges of sexism from the system, a wrong that depends on what was said between two people behind closed doors puts the victim on trial.

What ultimately saved the president and made my life easier was that the underlying lawsuit brought by Paula Jones was without merit. Even if everything she claimed were true, it did not amount to sexual harassment. Gross, crude, yes. But not sexual harassment. There was no abuse of power. By her own account, she was not coerced, and she was not penalized in any way for saying no. That is the line between public and private. The issue is not sex, but harassment. The consequences must be job-related. In the absence of any abuse of power, what happened in that room, like what happened in the Oval Office between the president and Monica Lewinsky, was private, and should have stayed that way.

There are two kinds of sexual harassment recognized by the courts, and Jones's accusations fit neither category, as the district judge ultimately ruled. The first, *quid pro quo* harassment, "this for that," deals with the situation in which job benefits are specifically tied to an employee's response to an unwelcome sexual advance. These are the cases in which abuse of power is most clear-cut, and economic coercion of sexual autonomy most easily recognized. Will you sleep with your boss to keep your job? Should economic power give an employer sexual power as well? The law against sexual harassment was supposed to limit that use of economic power.

But *quid pro quo* cases require the plaintiff to point to a specific employment decision that had been made because of her rebuff. Proving such a direct causal connection isn't easy even when it's there; most of us, after all, have at least one shortcoming, the equivalent of bad typing, which can be invoked as the "real" reason for a negative employment decision. Classic *quid pro quo* harassment leaves women who can't afford to say no without any protection at all; it leaves women who leave their jobs because they can no longer tolerate the conditions without recourse; and it leaves the women who are strong enough or desperate enough to put up with sexual harassment that the rest of us would never tolerate right where they are.

The second form of sexual harassment to be recognized was "hostile environment" harassment. In a hostile environment case, the plaintiff need not prove that any particular job-related benefit or detriment was conditioned on sex. What she must prove is that the harassment she faced was severe and pervasive; that it was unwelcome; and that not only did she find it offensive, but so would a reasonable person. The biggest problem with these cases is defining "it."

When I worked at the radio station KABC, I had a young assistant, a producer who became one of my "girls," my mentees, an army these days, and one that I am lovingly proud of. Sometimes, I called her "hon," or "sweetie," as in, "Listen, sweetie, here's what we need to do." Sometimes I touched her arm or shoulder. When I was working, I sent her to get me coffee. One day, I did all three at the same time. One of the other hosts, a conservative whom she didn't like, was there watching, and pounced. "If I'd just done that," he said to her, "you'd be screaming sexual harassment. Estrich does it and you ask if she wants milk in her coffee."

"If you did it, it *would* be sexual harassment," she replied, and left.

So he complained to me, instead. His argument was that it wasn't fair that I got to do things that he didn't, that what was acceptable conduct when I did it was unacceptable when he did it. Isn't that sex discrimination?

I told him that he could call me "hon" or "sweetie" anytime he wanted. I told him to touch my shoulder all he wanted. I told him that I'd be happy to get coffee for him if he was working or on-the-air and I wasn't.

And that's true. Compared to the stuff many of us put up with in the days before the law prohibited hostile environments, it was nothing. Besides, I was a secure, established, sometimes powerful forty-six-year-old, not a twenty-two-year-old in her first real job.

You're on a business trip. You finish a long day. The senior partner invites you to come by his room, have a beer, and watch the game. Appropriate? I ask my class. Half the women say yes. Half say no, unless they're romantically interested in him. Of course, none of the men have a problem with it. Would it matter if he were gay? The class turns silent. A gay man wouldn't do it.

Playboy pictures in your locker at the fire station? Everyone says fine. But what if you hang them up? What if you leave your locker door open? Free speech? We split again. Some people say it's offensive. Some people say it's protected speech under the First Amendment, a political statement about political correctness. Some people, which includes most of the men in the room, don't understand what the fuss is about.

A friend is at a business meeting with a senior man from her firm. The weather turns bad. There is only one room in the hotel where they are working. He suggests they share it. She doesn't like his tone and drives the two hours it takes to get home in the snow. She believes she has been sexually harassed. She refuses to work with this man again. A year later, she starts dating a partner in the firm, a man six years her senior. She is single. He is single. The management committee tells them that either they have to stop seeing each other, or one of them will have to leave the firm. She is infuriated. How dare they interfere with her private life?

A few years ago, a study found that while a majority of men said they would be flattered if a woman made sexual advances at work, a majority of women said they would be offended if a man did. Respected scholars have argued that the "reasonable person" whose evaluations of what counts as "severe" and "pervasive" as a matter of law is an implausible fiction: There are no reasonable people of a gender-neutral sort when it comes to sexual relations. There are only men and women. Experience teaches that when there is only one standard, it will be a male standard. The reasonable person in the public sphere long dominated by men is a reasonable man. Thus, it is argued, courts should apply sexual harassment law not according to the judgments of a reasonable person, but a reasonable woman. The liberal United States Court of Appeals for the Ninth Circuit was the first to adopt the reasonable woman standard as a matter of law, and there is currently a split among the circuit courts on whose perspective should govern.

But the reasonable woman raises almost as many issues as she resolves. Just who is this woman? Is she more like me or my young producer? How closely should she resemble the particular woman bringing the suit? In the criminal law, where reasonableness sets the threshold for negligence and recklessness liability, the debate about what characteristics of the defendant to apply to the reasonable person has been going on literally for centuries. There, the reasonable person is generally the same age as the defendant, the same height and weight, maybe even the same sex. But the law is less clear about whether the reasonable person also shares the defendant's life experiences and attitudes: Is she a battered woman or a duped husband? Does he or she come from the same culture, follow the same traditions, as the defendant?

If some women in the fire station don't mind the nudie pictures, and some do, how do we decide which of them is reasonable? Or should the question be, as it is in the criminal law, not what the women might have perceived, but what knowledge of the offense the men accused of wrongdoing can fairly be charged with?

If reasonable women are so different from their male equivalents that a separate legal standard is needed, then how are the men who are supposed to apply the standard—as workers and bosses, as judges and juries—to do it? Can only women serve on sexual harassment juries? Is it fair to punish a man for violating a standard that his gender precludes him from articulating?

There are easy answers, but no one likes them. You could prohibit all sexual relationships in the workplace, or all relationships between superiors and those over whom they have power. No sexual relationships between boss and secretary, partner and associate, student and teacher. This is what the military does. It is what codes of professional ethics for doctors and lawyers do.

But even if you bar all relationships between men in power and the women who work under them, you've only addressed half the problem. There is still the matter of the nude pictures, the crude jokes, the requests for coffee, the "honeys" and "dolls," the incidental brush against a woman's arm, or breast, and the question of whose perspective governs. Often, the two halves of sex-harassment law converge, with a plaintiff claiming both a prohibited *quid pro quo* and, even if she cannot prove the necessary causal relationship, a hostile environment.

Besides, most people don't want to be bound by the sort of absolute rules that govern in the military, or are supposed to. Both practical and principled concerns are regularly invoked, usually successfully, to avoid the general application of the rules that govern generals and servicewomen, doctors and patients, lawyers and clients.

The practical reason is that work is where you meet people; if you can't date people from work, who can you date? Work is a natural place to get to know a person as an individual before you judge him or her as a potential partner. You get a fuller picture than on a blind date. Many happy marriages began at work.

The principled reason is that it's nobody's business. The law of sexual harassment should protect personal autonomy, not constrict it. The argument based on personal autonomy is that I should be allowed to date—or sleep with—anyone I want, provided the other person is equally willing. For the employer to intrude when both parties have entered into a mutual relationship is a violation of that autonomy. It's one thing for an employer to set rules for what we do at work, as workers, and quite another for him or her to reach into our private space and lives.

You could require both parties to inform their superiors that they are dating and sign forms attesting to the fact that the relationship is welcome and consensual. My class titters when I suggest the idea (although some companies do require dating couples to sign a form agreeing not to sue), almost as much as they did when I proposed that a man and woman should both initial the condom package the first time they have sex, as a sign of consent. Getting it in writing is the law's traditional means of dealing with situations where misinterpretations are common and resolving them after the fact comes down to one person's word against another's. But when it comes to sex, it doesn't work.

Part of the personal autonomy we treasure is not only the doing, but the how; not only sex, but seduction; not only consummation, but also courtship. The idea that employers should regulate courtship offends many of us, almost as much as the notion that they have the right to prohibit the consummation.

Where that leaves us is in a world where two mock juries at a recent American Bar Association convention could hear the same case of alleged sexual harassment and one could find no liability at all and the other impose a multi-million dollar judgment. The workplace has changed dramatically. Even so, the problems of defining, and proving, sexual harassment still leave women feeling exposed and men confused, complicating the corporate culture to which women must find a way to adapt and generating its own mini-backlash.

A friend is the target of a complaint because he said that a woman looked good in black. To escape the possibility of punitive damages down the road, the company he has worked for all of his adult life removes him from the office so that she won't have to see him. He never asked the woman out, never touched her, was never alone with her, never saw her outside the office, never telephoned her—and he still had to move out of the office, across the street, and hire a lawyer. In the six months she worked as a clerk in the office, she never once complained to him or told him she felt uncomfortable. He didn't even like her. He chatted with her on occasion mostly because he felt sorry for her. As it turned out, he was lucky. She didn't lie. The incidents she recounted were so clearly insignificant that his lawyer advised him from the outset that he should be able to keep his job, which didn't totally reassure him. But she ultimately left, and he came back. He hopes that his company didn't pay her off, but who knows for sure? He still owes his lawyer legal fees.

Why didn't this woman just tell my friend to back off? In a much-publicized Pennsylvania case, the state Supreme Court reversed the rape conviction of a college student on the grounds that even though nonconsent had been established, there was no proof of force. The court emphasized that the woman made no effort to leave, even though she could have done so safely. Feminists raised the alarm bells that the resistance requirement was being smuggled back in. There are any number of reasons why a frightened woman might not attempt an escape, even if in retrospect it would have been safe. But was she frightened? Did she feel forced? Not according to the Court's version of the facts. And if she didn't feel frightened and didn't feel forced, why didn't she just leave?

A student came to my office recently to get my advice about how to deal with a male lawyer she believed was harassing her. She had worked at a small firm over the summer and was working part-time during her final year of law school. She expected to work there after graduation; now, she wasn't so sure, and with the interview season almost over, she was beginning to panic about her future. She described a man who was too attentive, too friendly, walked too close, made jokes she didn't find funny and sexual suggestions, supposedly in good humor, that struck her as anything but funny. "He's too interested in my personal life," she told me, "and it's none of his business. He wants a personal relationship, and I don't."

"Have you said anything to him?" I asked her. *It* had been going on for months. "Have you told him that you're offended?"

She hadn't. My guess is that he didn't have a clue. I found myself sympathizing with him.

What do we say to men who claim, with reason, to be caught in a generational vise, where conduct that is acceptable to women in their forties is unacceptable to women in their twenties—and no one is quite sure about the thirties. What makes these tales sympathetic is certainly not the desire some have for personal relationships with women half their age, but the fact that they can be the focus of a complaint for sexual harassment without even knowing that a woman was offended by their conduct.

My student wanted advice. Should she sue? Complain to the senior partner? Fling herself into the job market?

"Why don't you start by telling him you're not interested," I suggested. "Tell him you want a professional relationship, not a personal one. Tell him he's making you
uncomfortable. Before you charge a man with rape, scream
rape. Before you surrender, try to leave. Before you complain
of sexual harassment, tell him." There are some women who
would've enjoyed the attention, as long as it went no further
than that. Not her. Nor me, certainly not when I was her age.
There are some things that are so inappropriate that you
shouldn't have to be told not to do them. But at the margin,
in the generational vise, you can't blame a man for not knowing how you feel if you don't tell him.

The law against sexual harassment, like the law of rape,
gives women power to say no that we didn't have twenty
years ago. It's not a matter of persuasion; all you have to do is
say it. For men at work, the words "I consider this sexual
harassment" are almost as terrifying as the words "I consider
this rape." A man who keeps at it after he has been warned
deserves the consequences. That alone makes his own conduct more unreasonable; a reasonable person respects the way
others exercise their autonomy, even if his or her own
approach would be different.

A man who jumps out from behind bushes with an ice

pick in his hand will not be stopped by your informing him that you consider his actions to be rape. Of course it's rape. He knows that. It is what he intends. A man who takes pleasure in tormenting the women who work for him will not be stopped by their telling him that he is harassing them. That's the idea. But most men don't set out to rape; they want to have sex, consensual sex. Most men don't set out to engage in sexual harassment; they set out to flirt, they think they're being funny, they think the way they are behaving is okay. They would be terrified to know that you think they're violating the law. That is power that women never had before. You use it by telling them.

If saying no won't stop him, if no to some ears still means yes, say RAPE. Scream it at the top of your lungs. Make sure the neighbors hear. If telling a man to back off at work doesn't stop him, tell him that you're on your way to file a complaint for sexual harassment. Use the words. Title VII. A lawyer friend (me) was just mentioning it. Words have power. Rape and sexual harassment are powerful words. For most men, they are more than enough to replace ardor with terror.

General Kennedy's allegation was ultimately credited by the Army after the testimony of others whom she had told of the incident at the time. Her advice to women after her own experience is to complain promptly. Why not use our power well?

Writer Katie Roiphe has argued that feminist law reformers, instead of making women feel more powerful, have done just the opposite. The argument is that reformers are responsible for turning her generation into passive victims who would rather march with candles or file complaints than take responsibility for their lives and stand up for themselves. Now that they have the law to take care of them, they've forgotten how to take care of themselves.

I don't think carrying a candle signifies a permanent state of victimhood. If the term *rape* is sometimes used to refer to instances that the law wouldn't punish as such, so what; how many times do people say "I've been robbed," when the truth is that they have been taken advantage of. Nor is the issue whether it is one in nine or one in eight or even one in four; unless someone wants to argue that rape is not a problem worth addressing, that debate is strictly academic. The before and after rape statistics, showing much smaller increases in prosecution and conviction rates than might have been expected, are not the only measure, or even the best, of the impact of law reform. Law changes the texture of the society, provides the background rules to which most people adjust their behavior without the need for a prosecution or a lawsuit. In shifting the line between public and private, reform did more than increase the chances of success in close cases: It gave women power they didn't have, power they can and should use to protect themselves. The law is not a shield behind which a cowering generation can hide, or at least that's not how it has to be; it is a weapon in the arsenals of both self-esteem and self-protection.

Camille Paglia says women should be strong, should look out for themselves, should beware of fraternity houses. Of course. If the office lech is in the Xerox room, stay out of the Xerox room. Don't leave friends with drunken frat boys. Just because sexual abuse isn't our "fault" doesn't mean that women shouldn't do everything in our power to prevent it. Just because you don't have to resist doesn't mean you shouldn't fight back and win. Women should avoid situations where their autonomy is at risk, in the same way we avoid areas where crime is common, in the same way we lock our doors, and always wear our seat belts. If your house is burglarized after you forgot to lock your door, no one says the burglar has a right to the TV, but they do tell you to lock it next time.

"Where is your shirt?" I ask the student who comes up to me before class to tell me that she will have to leave early for a law firm interview. She is wearing a navy blue suit, but with a miniskirt, and no blouse underneath the jacket. In my day, it could've been a hundred degrees outside, and you wouldn't go to a law firm interview with nothing under your jacket. My student looks like she is dressed for a date. That is, in fact, how many of my students think of job interviews.

"How many of you flirt in law firm interviews?" I ask. The majority of women raise their hands. The rest are shocked. "It's like sports," one woman explains, a line I hear repeated often. Men come in and establish a bond about football. Successful athletes are much in demand at law firms, in the hopes that they can boost the firm's standing in the various leagues. "Guys like to be around good athletes and beautiful women," another student points out, which is almost certainly true. So should we practice our basketball shots, or buy miniskirts?

I received a phone call recently asking me to comment on a woman's decision to set up a scholarship fund that would give grants to female law students who are committed to following in Ally McBeal's footsteps and using their sexuality to succeed in law practice. "No shirt" grants, as it were. In the view of the donor, it is the only way for women to succeed and, therefore, should be encouraged. And she wasn't kidding.

The most traditional way for women to make men comfortable is, of course, by relating to them on a sexual basis; the most traditional, the most comfortable way for many men to relate to women is as objects of sexual desire. Of course there is power to be had for women in those relationships, particularly when all other avenues are closed off.

In a recent feature on the most successful women in business, *Fortune* magazine put the spotlight clearly on sexuality. What the women who made it to the top have in common, *Fortune* argued, was that they were attractive, feminine, and even a little bit sexy. This was *Fortune*'s conclusion, not mine. They wore pastel suits, knew how to flirt, and in one case, rumor had it, had even slept with the boss.

Monica Lewinsky got Vernon Jordan's help and the job she wanted at Revlon because she gave nine blow jobs to the President of the United States. She got his attention by flashing her thong underwear. Kathleen Willey got on the president's schedule on the very day she requested an appointment because she had flirted with him during the campaign. A man would have had to raise millions of dollars to get on that schedule; no male interns, to my knowledge, have commanded the attention of the president's best friend.

This is the other side of sexual power, the Lysistrata side, the province of the so-called "great dames" chronicled by Marie Brenner, the route to power when all others are closed. My generation put on blouses with bow ties at the neck in an effort to eliminate sex as an issue; the Ally McBeal–ites take theirs off altogether in an effort to use it as a draw.

Autonomy gives an individual the right to choose for herself, but it does not mean that all choices are equal. I am a feminist who wrote a diet book. I make no apologies for my belief that looking and feeling your best is almost certain to further your professional success; that there is probably not a woman alive, or not many, who doesn't do better, professionally speaking, when she feels good about herself; that most of us can remember just how we looked, and what we wore, on our most successful days; that being attractive helps, up to a point, in work situations; and that being overweight, unfairly but truthfully, is the kiss of death. I joke all the time that the reason for my success as a television pundette is not that I have run campaigns or taught law for twenty years, and thus might actually know what I am talking about, but that I have blonde hair and legs almost as good as those of the twenty- and thirty-something blondes with whom I'm usually paired. My gray-haired, size-fourteen Republican friends have no chance against a bevy of less-experienced but better-looking younger women who are the ones clearly favored by the middle-aged men who run the shows.

But sexuality takes you only so far. You don't run the world when you're on your knees. If sleeping your way to the top were the way to get there, secretaries would be running the world. The blondes rotate. They are interchangeable, expendable, and dangerous when desperate. The dames who are back in fashion had no other avenues available, and many of them were in it for the sport as much as need or ambition. Flirting with your dinner partner is different from flirting with your boss. In my own survey, more women have slept their way to the bottom than to the top.

An applicant in a mini-suit and no shirt may attract a man's eye, but she can ruin his career. Monica Lewinsky very nearly cost Bill Clinton the presidency. How many middle-aged men will trust their careers to Ally McBeal?

"I don't want to travel with a young female associate," more than one male partner has told me. "It makes me uncomfortable." Cynthia Fuchs Epstein found the same response in her research, as explained by one male partner: "When I'm on a transaction traveling, and we're in a hotel, if you're with a male associate, the deal is done, you can go to a room, and you turn on whatever—football game, basketball game, nerd films, whatever it is you want. . . . It's very hard to have that kind of camaraderie with a female associate. . . . You're just asking for problems down the road."

One of the most ridiculous moments of the last presidential campaign, one that would be funny were it not so troubling, was the press conference held by conservative candidate Gary Bauer to deny that he was having an affair with a young female staffer. What got Bauer into trouble was that he had spent time alone with this woman in his office and hers. After the press conference, it was reported that he was putting in clear glass petitions so no one could mistake a professional interaction for a personal one.

How many men in powerful positions will hire young women to be their traveling assistants?

I can make the case that there is a difference between women using their sexual power for economic gain and men using their economic power for sexual gain. The difference would be that men are starting out on top and women on the bottom; that men start out in a position of power, whereas the woman in that case is using what she has to get to where she can. I can make the case but I'm not sure I buy it. And it still doesn't make it a smart strategy when there are better routes available.

Clarence Thomas's supporters have accused liberal women's groups of using Anita Hill against him. Of course they're right. It wasn't the reason feminists first opposed Thomas, but at a time when the battle appeared to be lost, it was the only ammunition left.

It was the Senate Judiciary Committee's treatment of Anita Hill, as much as Clarence Thomas's, however, that enraged many women, myself included. In the first instance, reports that Thomas may have behaved improperly were summarily dismissed. Then, when news accounts forced the Senate to consider the charges, Anita Hill was treated the way rape victims have been for centuries. She was put on trial. The low point came when a man she knew only casually, who went on to have a career as a radio talk show host and might well have been auditioning for it on national television, was permitted to testify before the United States Senate and the country that Anita Hill had fantasies about a sexual relationship with him.

At the same time, Thomas played the race card, accusing Hill and her supporters of a "high-tech lynching of an uppity black." By doing so, he effectively put the all-white committee on the defensive; charges of racism carried far more weight than charges of sexism.

No one on either side ever stood up and said that even if everything Hill complained of was true, it only proved that Thomas was crude, not that he was a lawbreaker, or morally unqualified to serve on the Supreme Court. The Republicans didn't say it because men who hold themselves out as the representatives of morality and family values are easily trapped by the hypocrisy of their high-mindedness. Crusaders against pornography cannot easily dismiss Long Dong Silver jokes as merely tasteless. Instead, they feigned shock and disgust, adopting the position that if the charges were true, they would certainly doom Thomas.

Feminists, determined to defeat Thomas, took the same position, which is what came back to haunt many of us years later, when the issue was not crude jokes but sex between the president and an intern. If the former should disqualify a man from serving on the Supreme Court, shouldn't the latter dis-qualify him from serving as president?

It was said at the time that Clarence Thomas had a special responsibility to treat women fairly precisely because his job was to head the agency charged with enforcing Title VII. That is surely true, but it is hard to argue that the President of the United States should be subject to a lower standard than the men who work under him.

If you believe Hill, as I always have, Thomas made off-color remarks in her presence, the most memorable ones being his reference to pubic hair in a Coke can and Long Dong Silver. Tasteless, to be sure. But sexual harassment? Enough to stop a man from being confirmed? No. I think the verdict the country has reached on Clarence Thomas is that Anita Hill was telling the truth, but that it wasn't bad enough to block him from serving.

The "reasonable woman" or "person" sets the threshold for liability. She or it is the external standard, that protects a man from being sued by a hypersensitive woman. But we don't regulate sex the way we do chemicals in the workplace, setting across-the-board standards and enforcing them that way. The purpose of recognizing sexual harassment as a form of sex discrimination was to protect the exercise of sexual autonomy, which includes the right to say yes to another willing adult, as well as the unilateral right to say no.

Monica Lewinsky wasn't trapped, at least not by the president. His advances were not only welcome, they were invited. She went after him. If you believe Anita Hill, then Clarence Thomas knew that Hill was uncomfortable and didn't care; far from caring, he may have even taken some pleasure in her obvious embarrassment, which is far more damning than anything he said. If you believe Monica Lewinsky, it was she, and not the president, who introduced sexuality into their relationship. He did not abuse his power. He did not coerce her to have sex. She did not feel oppressed by a hostile environment. The president should have known better. They were both foolish. It was certain to be a disaster. It was totally inappropriate. But it's private.

It's Gloria Steinem and me against two young conservative blondes, the interchangeable ones who make their living damning sex in short skirts. They regularly appear on television without shirts. They are horrified by the relationship between the president and Monica Lewinsky. "But what about the fact that it was consensual?" Gloria asks. "What about the fact that she may have initiated it; that it was her choice?" "Irrelevant," one of the conservatives argues.

"Beside the point," the other agrees. What difference does consent make? All the difference in the world.

Autonomy is the right to make your own mistakes, to use your power, even poorly, so long as you do not use it to trample another person's autonomy. I have fought for two decades to give women and men the power to choose for themselves, even if I sometimes disagree with the choices they make.

NINE

Political Power

The Vice President of the United States is yelling at me on the telephone. He is furious. I have betrayed him. Our relationship will never be the same. How could I do this to him? I hate being yelled at. I yell back. I am writing a book about women and power, and I am trying to wield it. It is working, but it isn't fun.

For months, I had been trying in my usual nice and polite way to convince the campaign chiefs of the front-runner for the Democratic nomination for president that they needed more women at the table. My old friend Ann Lewis, the senior woman at the White House, and I have taken this up as our little project, something neither of us can quite believe we actually have to do in 1999. But we do. The Gore campaign is being viewed by insiders as a battle of the princes—a long list of current and former Gore staffers and allies, all of them white men, most of them now lobbyists in Washington—who are his chief strategists, advisers, and fund-raisers. Most observers are trying to figure out which prince will win; Ann and I are trying to figure out why it's only princes. Between us, we have talked to most of them about the need to get some women to the table. They take my calls, they couldn't be nicer; these are guys I know and like, and I went to bat for them when there was "no controlling legal authority" and Gore was under attack for fund-raising improprieties. But both Ann and I, and the other women we know who are calling, are getting put off repeatedly; they have told us to be patient, just wait, they'll get to that. In the meantime, Bill Bradley has hired my friend Gina Glantz, a fifty-three-year-old woman no less, as his campaign manager, and women across the country are regularly being called by Gina. The Gore campaign should be doing the same thing, but there is no one to do it, which is good for Gina, but bad for the party, which is still likely to nominate Gore, who can only win with women. I try making this case to the men I talk to: that they need women not just because they look good in photo opportunities, but because Democrats don't win without their votes, and having women at the table is related to waging the sort of campaign that wins women's votes at the ballot box. Be patient, I'm told.

In the meantime, the Democratic Party, controlled by the vice president, chooses Los Angeles as the site for its convention. And even though many of us have been saying very explicitly to anyone who would listen that if there's one thing they shouldn't do, it is to have a group of rich white men announce that they are hosting a convention in Los Angeles, that is exactly what they do. It's another picture to add to my growing collection. There is a new joke in town: The Gore campaign's idea of affirmative action is finding five white guys in the most diverse city in America. I am not laughing.

Two years ago, the Hollywood Women's Political Committee disbanded. The organization of women from the entertainment industry was much mocked by some in political circles, but it was also respected because of the wealth of the women involved. It disbanded because many of its members were disgusted at being part of what they came to see as the essentially corrupt business of buying politicians with private money, and many of them found it difficult to participate in a system and seek to change it at the same time. "Do we need to get some rich women together so the boys will pay attention to getting women to the table?" I ask my best-connected women friends in Washington. I want them to say no. They say yes. I report back to my West Coast friends, who are disappointed that in order to get to their table, we have to create another one of our own. Is this really 1999?

I call one of Gore's top aides. I tell him that my friend Lynne Wasserman, whose family has given more money to Democratic politicians than any other in Southern California (or maybe America; they are at least in the top three) is considering forming a new caucus of Democratic women, comprised of wealthy and media-savvy women, whose sole purpose will be to assure that there are women at the table in the presidential campaigns and at the convention. I tell him that she already has a list of ten or more women who are eager to be charter members (everyone she and I have had lunch with that week). A dinner is planned for Friday night, where I expect the group to come together. It can still be stopped with swift action by the Gore campaign to address the problems in their campaign and in the convention committee. "I'll get back to you," the aide says.

Weeks pass. "When are you going to write a column

announcing our new group?" Lynne asks me. "They won't pay attention until they read it in the paper." It is hard to disagree. I get calls from women telling me that they are being jerked around by the princes in their efforts to get involved in the campaign, promises made and ignored, short lists formed and unformed. Other women call to say they hear I'm doing something to take on the white boys running the Gore campaign and to be sure to use their names. I place more calls to the campaign.

I finally get a return call. I say that Lynne is ready to go forward with the group, that the convention announcement, and the inertia since, have broken the camel's back, and that I am prepared to write a column about the new group. The aide is not happy. By now, I am taking notes. "What women do you have at the table?" I ask repeatedly. He gets defensive. He tells me that they do have "a woman" at the table, Elaine Kamarck, and that while "she might not be your kind of woman," she is a woman. "Call her," he tells me.

In fact, Elaine Kamarck is an old friend of mine. What he means when he says that she is not "my kind of woman" is that Elaine has always defined herself as a conservative Democrat, a Sam Nunn Democrat, the representative of the Democratic Leadership Council at the table, not the Women's

Council. She is not connected, even informally, to the organized women's community in Washington. She doesn't do the feminist piece, which would be fine if there were someone else doing it.

Elaine also lives in Boston and teaches at Harvard, which, the last time I checked, is not where the presidential campaign headquarters are located. I call her anyway. I tell her what I'm working on. She has just that moment been e-mailed the latest piece from *U.S. News and World Report* listing the insiders in the campaign, fourteen men and her. What's worse, the story—which is clearly coming from inside the campaign— suggests that her role as the head of issues is being shared with another Harvard professor and old friend of mine, Christopher Edley; in fact, the story suggests that he's the one running the show, and that she's working for him. The notion that the one black and the one woman in the senior ranks of the campaign are fighting for the same seat at the table appalls both of us. Can this be what the princes had in mind when they suggested I call Elaine? She has no complaints about her relationship to the candidate, but she offers no defense of the princes. She e-mails me the story.

I write a column connecting the need for women as voters with the need to have women at the table, pointing to the

reported underrepresentation of women in the Gore campaign and connecting it to the fact that Gore was not pulling
women's votes against Bush in the numbers Democrats must
in order to win. The lead was pointed: "Al Gore may turn out
to have a bigger problem with women than his boss. But in
Gore's case, the problem is professional."

I don't send the column to my syndicate, or to *USA Today,*
which has already offered to run a piece on "Al Gore's woman
problem" sight unseen. One last try. I send it overnight mail
to the vice president himself. And I place a call to him, making
it clear that I want to speak to the vice president himself, not
to one of the princes. Two days pass. No word.

USA Today wants to run the piece on the following Monday. But there is a problem. On Monday, I am taking my children to the Easter Egg Roll at the White House. Then we're
spending the night there.

I first got to know the vice president when he ran against
my candidate, Governor Dukakis, in 1988. In the close circle
of presidential campaigns, Gore's was the least popular; all the
campaign managers got along except his, and his New York
campaign was particularly unattractive. But I had occasion to
see Al Gore again when he was on a promotional tour for his
book about the environment, after his son had nearly been

killed in an accident, and he impressed me greatly. When, as vice president, he came under investigation for supposedly making illegal fund-raising calls, I jumped to his defense—on television, and in print, over and over. He sent me nice notes thanking me. I cohosted a dinner party for him, during the 1994 campaign, at the request of a former student and friend of mine, who was then his political director. I saw him socially once or twice a year. We always kissed hello. I wanted him to like me. I hate confrontation. I like to be liked by everybody, to be seen as a team player and not an ambitious chick.

But I was also writing a book about power and even I could see that my strategy was impotent. If I sent the column in after I was entertained at the White House, I would look ungrateful; if I didn't, it would look like I'd been bought off. The only thing to do was to send it in and let the chips fall. I told my children that we might be uninvited, but this was a matter of principle, and power. I sent the column to my syndicate.

Two days later, Al Gore called to yell at me, which is what turned the column into a story. I don't know if any of the papers who took my column ever bothered to run it; a reporter for one of them called me months later to ask for a copy of the confidential "memo." Op-ed pages tend to be run by conservative white men, most of whom don't have many women on their staffs either. If they have one female columnist, they think that's plenty. So what if Al Gore is no better.

But the vice president yelling at me is a story that made it to the gossip columns and the Sunday talk shows, and excerpts of my "secret memo" ran in the New York tabloids. I never wrote about it, until now, even though I could have, if my goal had been to hurt the vice president, as he initially claimed. But that wasn't my goal at all. I think he'll be a terrific president. I want to make sure he is as good as he can be, that he is surrounded by the very best, women and men. The lesson in this story is not only about how hard it is to wield power, but also how easy. This is what happened next.

I hang up from my call with the vice president. I am shaking. I am also about to get on a plane to Washington with my family. I propose that we go to the beach instead. The vote is three to one in favor of going to Washington. We arrive in Washington Thursday night, in time for the president's radio address on Friday, to which we have also been invited. They send the details to the hotel. So far, so good, I guess; we haven't been disinvited. We go to the White House, where we are directed to the Roosevelt Room. The war in Kosovo is in its second week. The president is running late. I am judging the reactions of everyone I see. Are they all mad at me? Is this what it takes to be powerful?

Ann Lewis comes upstairs to find me. When the vice president finished yelling at me, he called her. He claimed to both of us that this was the first he'd heard that anyone thought he had a problem with women in his campaign, which seems to me, but not to him, a plain indictment of his own campaign. I ask Ann if she yelled back. She says no. She works there. Her advice is that I ask the president to get involved. I find this rather horrifying. There is a war in Kosovo. Does she think things are so bad that I need to get the president involved in my dispute with the vice president about the number of women in his campaign? Today? Not even waiting until Monday, when we'll be spending the night and it might be easier. She does. Why didn't he just ask me to help him find some women for the campaign? He could've co-opted me in a minute. Instead, if I take Ann's advice, I'm about to involve the president. My stomach is churning.

We wait two hours. I avoid going anywhere near the vice president's office. We finally go in to listen to the radio address, after which each family group has its picture taken with the president. I force my children, who are tired from waiting, to wait longer, positioning them at the end of the line, so I'll have time to talk to the president.

Finally, it is our turn. He kisses me hello, takes my hand, couldn't be warmer. Clearly, he's not mad at me. "I have a little problem," I say. "Your friend, the vice president, is mad at me."

His answer stuns me. Later, I will laugh.

"I know," says the President of the United States. He laughs. "He came in to me this morning to complain about you, and I said, 'Al, stop *ka-vetching* about Susan. She's just trying to help.' "

The president tells me that he's going to try to solve the problem. "You know, you're right," he says. "It is a white boys' campaign. They do need women." Besides, he thought the line about Gore having a bigger problem with women than he did was pretty funny.

Wipe me off the floor. A column that has yet to be published has now gotten the attention of the president and the vice president. All it took was the possibility of it being published, and the willingness to endure a stomachache, and people being mad at me. I tell *USA Today* that events have overtaken the piece, and I won't be submitting it.

The vice president and I made up two weeks later. I

wrote him a note, not apologizing, but explaining why inclusion is so important in a twenty-first-century campaign, why the debate has to move beyond questions of conscious discrimination, of who did what to whom, to the more important challenge of how we include everyone at the table; that it's not a matter of justice, but of a winning strategy; of strength not charity. I don't know what the president said, but the vice president called me four times on the next Saturday, and talked to my husband, my daughter, and my answering machine before we finally connected. He said it was important to him that we talked. Clearly. "He must want something," I said to Lynne. He wanted me to know that I was right about the need for diversity and that he thought of us as friends. My stomach suddenly felt better.

He told me about the calls he'd made to diversify the convention. He asked me what I thought of Donna Brazile, the African-American woman who was being considered for a job as political director.

I fired Donna Brazile in 1988 for speaking out in violation of the candidate's direct instructions about rumors surrounding George Bush's personal life.

"She could run your campaign," I said.

She does now.

This is a great place to end the story, but of course, it isn't that simple. Even her harshest critics acknowledge that Donna Brazile has made a difference at the table. Her advice is different, her perspective is different, and it is needed. But since the time of her appointment, there's been backtalk that she really doesn't run the campaign, isn't in charge, is just there because she's a black woman. What makes this worse is the fact that the Democratic Party made no bones about the fact that it wanted a Hispanic woman to be CEO of the convention. This story would be funny, if it weren't so painful: A senior party official called to tell me that a Hispanic woman would be running the convention. I said, "Great, who?" He said, "I don't know. Do *you* know anyone?" I didn't. Neither did anyone else. The woman who was finally selected was a talented field organizer with no experience in national political conventions. She had a very difficult time. Ultimately, Terry McAuliffe—reportedly the initial choice to run the convention before I made my stink—came in to rescue it, and Donna remains the only woman at the table.

When I asked the men organizing the Democratic convention in Los Angeles why the leaders of the host committee were all men, their answer was simple: They were the ones willing to put up the money. It is not that there are no rich women in Los Angeles; there are many. Indeed, depending on whose numbers you believe, women control a minimum of almost half the wealth in the country and, because they tend to live longer, ultimately as much as 90 percent flows through their hands. When it comes to household purchases, women make 80 percent of the decisions. Part of the problem in politics is the self-fulfilling prophecy that men tend to seek the help of other men, particularly those who owe them, those with whom they do business; political fund-raising is strictly a networking operation, and when there are men on top, there are more likely to be men at every level.

But you can't just blame it on the men. The other half of the problem is the women; it's about us, too. My friend Stanley Gold, a powerful Los Angeles businessman who has raised money for numerous causes and candidates, points out that when you ask a wealthy woman for a $1,000 contribution for a political campaign or cause, the most likely response you will hear is, "I have to ask my husband." These are women who can afford it; women who spend much more in an afternoon at Neiman Marcus without asking anyone's permission, indeed, often without even telling their husbands after the fact. These are women who make much more costly decisions about furnishings, home improvements, wardrobes, knick-knacks, travel, and maintenance, without checking with any-one; women who run their husband's lives in most respects, manage the family's budget, make the much more important judgments about children and family without asking anyone's permission—and yet won't write a check to a candidate for $1,000 without asking permission. As Stanley points out, "If they're going to ask their husbands, you might as well ask him in the first place." In my own informal survey, by the way, I have only found one man who says that he asks his wife before writing a check to a candidate.

EMILY's List, founded by activist Ellen Malcolm to sup-port progressive female candidates by bundling the contribu-tions of women, has emerged as one of Washington's biggest and most successful political action committees. Early Money Is Like Yeast is the slogan of EMILY's list; for years, women didn't have access to money early enough in a campaign to establish credibility and raise more money. EMILY's List makes an enormous difference for candidates seeking to demonstrate early credibility. But there is only one EMILY's list, and there are literally hundreds of political action com-mittees dominated by men.

According to a study by Professors John Green, Paul

Hernson, Lynda Powell, and Clyde Wilcox, among those who contributed $200 or more to Senate and House candidates, the percentage of women increased from 17 percent in 1978 to 23 percent in 1996. That is, to be sure, a significant increase. But the fact remains that 77 percent of the donors are men.

The same study found that women contributors differ from men in significant respects that shape our politics. Women were more likely to be democrats, more likely to hold liberal positions on issues like abortion, taxes, and the environment, and more likely to be motivated to give by policy concerns than because of business or employment reasons. These are the views that are underrepresented in the financial arms race.

Ask a politician who his best friends are and, without a pause, most of them will reel off the names of the people who contribute and raise the most money for them. This is what friendship is in a business where everyone is convinced that a war chest is key to survival and success. Even congressmen in safe seats want to have a million dollars in the bank. There are no party bosses any more; organizers count for far less than donors. The national committees of the two parties are little more than fund-raising operations; party leaders aren't leaders, they are fund-raisers; supporters don't give support, they give money; and lip service notwithstanding, it is the people who can give large sums and raise it, not the small donors everyone likes to brag about, whose calls get returned and whose bidding gets done. Money brings access and influence. In politics, money is power, and by a three to one ratio, men have it.

Incumbency is the electoral version of the old boys' network. When women do run for an open seat, most experts say that they have just as good a chance of winning as men, and there have even been some surveys to back that up. But open seats in Congress are a rarity. The hardest thing in congressional politics is getting there in the first place. Once you're there, it's easy to stay forever, as many men do. Advocates of term limits argue that they are in fact a bonanza for women because they create open seats on a regular basis: State legislatures with term limits have more women in them than legislatures that don't, but men still dominate. Incumbency is clearly an obstacle to women's success in politics, but it doesn't explain it all away.

It is also about us. Nationally, the number of women running for state legislatures has actually been dropping. In 1998, 2,279 women ran for state legislative positions—almost 100 fewer than in 1992. While the number of women in legislatures has increased substantially in three decades, it has leveled off in the low twenties, percentage-wise, with no increase in recent elections. Most women's political groups are also shrinking: The League of Women Voters is half the size it was in 1970.

Women who do run may find themselves confronting the same sorts of conscious and unconscious assumptions that women in corporate America do, particularly when they seek an executive office. Since the first woman was elected as a governor in 1925, sixteen women in all have served as governors of fourteen states; Texas and Arizona are the only states to have had two women, and thirty-six states have never had one. Sound like the Fortune 500? Moreover, the count of sixteen overstates women's success, since it includes two women who campaigned and were elected as surrogates for their husbands, one who won a special election to complete her deceased husband's term but then lost when she ran for a full term, two who had been secretaries of state and were sworn in when the elected governor was unable to complete his term, and one who served for nine days between the time the sitting governor was sworn in to the United States Senate and the governor-elect was sworn in to replace him. Currently, there are three women governors serving in office, a total of 6 percent; 8 percent—or four—is the highest it has ever been at any one time, from January to March 1991, and in 1994. Eight percent is again the magic number.

Professor Kathy Dolan has studied support for women candidates by gender for different levels of offices and has found a gender gap that increases as the level of office does. Using a population of college students, Professor Dolan found that 92 percent of the men and 96 percent of the women were willing to support a candidate for local office. Among the women, 3 percent said they were unsure whether they would support a woman, and 1 percent said they would not. These percentages remained exactly the same when the female students were asked whether they would support a woman for state office and for national office; they changed only when the question was support for a woman president, with 80 percent of the women saying they would support a woman, 16 percent unsure, and 4 percent saying no. Men, by contrast, were less supportive of women candidates above the level of local office. For state office, 13 percent of the men were either unsure or said no outright; for national office, 18 percent were either unsure or said no outright; for president, a whopping 46 percent of the men said that they were unsure or simply said no. These figures are particularly striking because this was an audience of college students, not randomly selected voters, which should make them more prone to support female candidates, both because they are younger and because they are better educated. Moreover, every one of these students must have known that the politically correct answer was to say yes, regardless of what one might actually do in the ballot booth, suggesting that if anything, the hostility toward women running for office was understated in Dolan's work.

Particularly among women. The female college students in Dolan's work overwhelmingly disclaimed any bias against female candidates for local or state office, but even among college women, one in five weren't sure they could vote for a woman for president. The perception that women vote for women is greater than the reality. In its year 2000 "Women in Leadership Poll," Deloitte & Touche reported that almost two-thirds of the public believe that women are more likely to vote for female political candidates than their male counterparts. Not so. There is scant evidence of an advantage for Republican women and only a modest one for Democrats, suggesting that ideology and party may be the controlling factors. A 1989 study done by EMILY's List found that "many women voters remained hesitant about supporting women candidates" and that "there is no 'leg up,' no advantage, with women voters [for female candidates]." Or as Christine Todd Whitman told *Fox News*'s Paula Zahn, "men elect women."

"Too ambitious," one the most ambitious women I know says, and I stop laughing when I realize she is serious.

"She should have left him," a friend struggling to keep her own marriage together says. "Or at least found a way to get even in public."

Just how tough women can be on other women was brought home in the opening days of Hillary Clinton's campaign, when the early polls revealed that she had a "woman problem" of her own. And not just any woman problem. Among suburban white women of her own generation, Hillary Clinton was running twenty points behind New York's tough-talking mayor, Rudy Guiliani. The women who saved her husband from impeachment by standing by him (even though they were among those most offended by his conduct) were not standing by Hillary.

There are any number of perfectly good reasons not to support Hillary Clinton for Senate that have absolutely nothing to do with gender. But what is striking in all the efforts to explain Hillary's "woman problem" is just how personal it is. It is not really about ideology or geography; almost no one says anything about competence. They talk about life choices: hers and ours, and what hers say about ours, which is certainly not how we usually judge male politicians.

I happen to know Hillary. She is just as smart as everyone assumes, but she is also warmer, funnier, and plain nicer than her public image. She's one of these women you meet and say, This is a woman who's a lifelong friend. She wears well— the better you know her, the more you like her.

But most people don't know her; they certainly didn't know her last spring, when the news media entered its frenzy about Hillary Clinton. What women were talking about was not the person, but the idea of Hillary Clinton.

The idea of Hillary Clinton is the idea of a woman who puts career first; who will do anything, put up with anything, sell her soul if necessary to keep her hands on the levers of power. "There are some people who don't like ambitious women and they ain't going to vote for her," James Carville said. "We've lost 'em. Never had 'em. Not going to get 'em."

Of course there's Madeleine Albright, in many ways far more powerful than Hillary, and the most popular member of the Clinton cabinet. Rooting for Madeleine is easy. Her rise to power came after her college sweetheart left her for a younger woman and after her daughters were adults. Older than most of the men she worked for, she hung in there when others might have given up and paid every penny of her dues, and then some. Whereas in the 1980s, the boys' foreign policy priesthood wouldn't invite her to the soirees they held for visiting foreign policy potentates, today, she presides at state dinners. It's a fairy tale told by Fay Weldon. The personal is political.

Hillary is a trickier heroine. She isn't looking for a prince, or recovering from losing one. She seems content to use the frog for all he's worth, which is hardly the fairy tale we grew up with. The only thing worse than the notion that she loves him despite it all is the idea that she doesn't and that all she's cared about from the beginning is getting power. Her happy ending seems to be only about winning. To want power that badly—to make the political personal—is not something most women empathize with. It's not the choice we made. But it is precisely for that reason that we need to support other women who live their lives differently.

The Equal Rights Amendment was defeated not by men but by women. The genius of Phyllis Schlafly was to convince traditional women that they would pay for the equality that working women were demanding, to pit the women against the ladies. The women were wrong to let it happen, and the ladies were wrong to believe it. It was a lose-lose proposition.

Not every woman who gets elected to office cares about the issues that most women do; there are men who do more to support families than women. And there is no reason a woman should feel constrained to vote for a candidate with whom she has fundamental disagreements, simply because she is a woman.

But is there any doubt that a Senate half-comprised of Hillarys would do more to further the agenda of the suburban women who question her values than the one we have now?

Should we judge Hillary on her public agenda or her private life? The choices we make about staying married and raising children are private, or they should be.

In one report on National Public Radio, a group of suburban women had been gathered to talk about Hillary Clinton. After listening to the conversation, the reporter asked whether the women were setting the bar very high for her. One of the women answered, "I think being a woman, the bar's always set higher for us. We cannot function like men do and get to the same place because we would be called bitches and avaricious and everything else. So, yes, the bar is set higher, but I think we've all had that in business. And why shouldn't she be held to the same standard we are?"

Instead of seeing our common agenda, we are eating our best alive. Most of us would never dream of running for Senate were we in Hillary's shoes, which is one of the reasons there are so few women in high elective office. It takes a level of ambition that most of us don't have. But that should be a reason for supporting those who do, not for opposing them.

An issue is something with two sides. I was called one day by a booker for a news network, who asked me whether I was free at 3:00 P.M. (the most important question) and whether I was for or against affirmative action. I explained my position: opposed to quotas, in favor of outreach, in favor of goals where there is a documented history of discrimination or an important need for diversity. The booker was impressed. She said I was the most sensible person she'd talked to all day. I pointed out that my position was probably the only one that you could square with the Supreme Court's rulings. "Well that's certainly important," she said. "But does it make you for or against affirmative action?" I said I was against affirmative action except in those rare cases where I was for it. She said they were only having two guests on that day.

It's easy to pit the the men against the women, the women against the ladies, the feminists against each other. If you're in the entertainment business, which most news organizations are, pitting the whackball on the left against the whackball on the right will at least keep people awake during the segment. "We really need you to mix it up on this one," you're told. "Feel free to interrupt. . . ." It even works for candidates sometimes, where the goal is to get 51 percent of a shrinking electorate; it doesn't matter how few people vote if you get one more than the other person.

But there are other ways to do battle. When women cross the predictable lines of party, or neighborhood, or class, or employer, or division, when we don't fall for divide-and-conquer, that alone conveys power. When the women in Congress decide to work together, nothing can stop them. Tokens who speak up cannot be ignored, or fired. They can insist on not being the only woman in the room. Get one powerful man to join three less-powerful women in making a request, and watch how seriously you are taken.

Men dominate politics not because they have more to say, but because they think they do. We give it to them. We don't act as women. We don't use the power that comes when people act collectively to further their collective interests.

As Wendy Kaminer explains, feminism has always had a collectivist element and an individualist element. The individualist element holds out the promise that any woman, and any man, can be whoever they want. The collectivist element is the route to getting there: the recognition that people who start out less powerful become equal by acting together; that it is through union and not division, by finding and acting on the issues that affect us as women, that we use our power. We can run ourselves, or support women who do. We can give them money without asking for permission. We can demand a seat at the table, or get them for each other. We can demand that candidates answer our questions, attend our forums, respond to our concerns—or find a woman to run against those who don't. The problem is not what we can do, but what we will do.

I have always hated conflict. I know many women do. Sometimes this works to our advantage and to society's. But as any good storyteller will tell you, you need conflict if you want things to change. Avoiding conflict is running in place. I am told that there are some inside the Gore campaign who are still afraid of me. So be it. Sometimes it is better to be feared than loved. Sometimes, all it takes to wield power is the willingness to be yelled at and an ample supply of Tums.

TEN

Changing   Ourselves

My friend is a powerful businesswoman. She doesn't run the company, but she's closer to it than any other woman. She has gone as far as any woman has in her business. And what does her fifteen-year-old daughter want to be when she grows up? "A mother," she says. "Isn't that enough?"

My friend is one of those women who never seems to waste time, races home for dinner, and serves on all the school committees. Rebellion is easier to recognize in someone else's daughter. But is this rebellion?

I have a theory. I think my friend is a great mother. My guess is her daughter would agree. Sorry to the conservatives, but I don't hear the voice of a neglected child, cast aside by her ambitious mother. Not at all. It's more about how hard her mother's life looks to her.

For those of us who looked at our mothers' lives and saw Betty Friedan's "feminine mystique" gone wrong, it's time to ask what our daughters see when they look at us. Exhaustion? Stress? Guilt? Frustration? My friend loves to be a mother, there is no doubt of that. So do I. Our children know that. We tell them that we would like to be with them more, and that is true. But we also love our work. We need that, too.

I am moderating a moot court debate between two of Los Angeles's premier attorneys. Both are senior partners in major law firms. One of the attorneys has brought her eleven-year-old son to the debate; she has two younger sons at home. I had considered bringing my eight-year-old—I had barely seen her that day—until I realized how late we would be there. I chat with the boy while his mother is in the ladies' room. "Do you want to be a lawyer?" I ask him. "No way," he replies. "My mom hates her job." Hates her job? One of the very top female lawyers in our city, probably the top female litigator downtown? "Does she really?" I ask. "It causes her so much stress," he says. I'm sure it does. But she also loves it. I can tell just by watching her do it.

It is hard to be a woman in what is still a man's world. There are days when every feminist jokes that we must have had it wrong, that this could not possibly be what we fought a revolution for. Did we win or lose? we ask one another. There are days when every woman yearns to be taken care of, protected, judged by her apple pie. But we know better. On television, the Nelsons lived happily ever after. In real life, Ozzie was a tyrant, and Harriet had no choice but to put up with him.

We have taught our children that motherhood is a miracle. The version of feminism that saw the burden and not the blessing, the unfairness and not the fulfillment, the limits and not the possibilities, was wrong. We may not have wanted to be our mothers, but most of us who discovered feminism twenty years ago also discovered that motherhood had been sold short; those of us who were lucky, blessed, discovered it in time. The message we are sending, very clearly, is that being a mother matters, and it does. But motherhood doesn't need a movement anywhere near as desperately as ambition does. Hallmark celebrates women who are mothers; who celebrates women who want power?

What about the sense of power and possibility that comes with the realization that *what is* is not inevitable, that the struggle is larger than you, that change is possible? Have we taught our daughters that? Do they even have any idea what that means?

And our sons. Dare we ask? Have you ever heard a boy answer "a father" when someone asks him what he is going to be when he grows up? Of course little boys want to be fathers. But that is not what they are going to *be*, not what they are going to *do*. "I'd love to stay home and raise the kids," one of my older students, a dad already, tells me. "But my wife expects me to go out and earn a living. She wants to stay home. I have no choice."

On the first day of kindergarten last year, the boys and girls in my son's class immediately divided for free play. The girls gathered at the art tables to color with markers. The boys gathered at the computers to go on math adventures.

Boys and girls come differently. My son was born hardwired to turn sticks into guns, fight bad guys with swords, and chase girls. He likes to play with wires. My daughter is working on a story about a girl superhero named Marigold who has the special power to stop fights. She's always liked dolls.

But whatever the innate differences, there is no question that we raise our children differently according to their sex.

Even feminist mothers do it, consciously as well as unconsciously, justifying ourselves by our desire that our children
should fit in. Girls dress up as Peter Pan every Halloween, but
have you ever seen a little boy dressed up as Tinker Bell? I
once asked my radio listeners if any of them would allow their
sons to wear a "girl's" costume for Halloween, and the
response was overwhelmingly negative.

In doing so, we reinforce the view that what the boys have
is better. When my daughter was five, she wore black sneakers
to Sunday school, where she was teased for wearing "boys'
sneakers." The truth is, ever since my son was born, I had
encouraged the reds and blacks over the pinks and purples,
since I'd get more wear out of them. "What did you say?" I
asked her. "I told them girls could wear anything boys could,"
she replied. Such a mother I am. "Can boys wear anything
girls can?" she asked. "Not exactly," I said. "But that's not fair
to boys," my daughter replied. "Don't they want to wear
girls' colors? Don't they get mad?" No. They grow up believing theirs are better.

Eventually, as I stand watching, I notice one girl at the
computer table playing with the boys. While it is true that
boys and girls are different, it is also true that we all are a com-
bination of traits. Some girls like computers and some boys

hate them. The point of prohibiting sex discrimination was to free both men and women, both girls and boys, from the constraints imposed by even accurate stereotypes. It was to let girls do computers and to let boys draw.

That's easy. But what if most of the girls keep drawing? What if we declare that sports funding shall now be fifty-fifty, boys and girls, and more boys sign up than girls? Does it matter if it's nature or nurture, if it shapes where they're headed?

"I don't feel powerful," Ogilvy & Mather CEO Shelly Lazarus told *Fortune* magazine upon being named number four on their 1998 list of the fifty most powerful women in American business. "Power is more important to men," she says. "Men like to issue orders. They like to feel powerful. I get no thrill out of being powerful." Jill Barad, who was number six on the list until she was replaced as Mattel's CEO, would have preferred to be on a list of the most interesting women. "When you apply the word 'power' to a man, it means strong and bold—very positive attributes. When you use it to describe a woman, it suggests bitchy, insensitive, hard." Ann Winblad, Silicon Valley's leading software venture capitalist and number twenty-four on the list, describes power as "a very dangerous word." Abby Joseph Cohen, widely viewed as the most powerful woman on Wall Street, disclaims any personal power. "The power belongs to the analysis," she says, and describes herself as "just recognizing and summarizing" the reasons supporting a bull market. Very few powerful men talk this way.

Then there is the matter of future plans for the most powerful women in business. Heidi Miller, chief financial officer of Citigroup and number three on the list, doesn't dream of being president of Citigroup; her fantasy career goal is to be president of Princeton. Sherry Lansing, who runs Paramount Pictures, dreams of running a foundation for cancer research. Rebecca Mark of Enron, one of the few women who actually is comfortable talking about power, would like to "live in my house in Taos, ski every day, and raise my horses." She has no desire to be CEO of Enron or any other big company. "I'm getting old," says the forty-four-year-old.

In recent years, business magazines, executive consultants, and economic forecasters have reported on a trend of women dropping out, not only because of their children, but because they simply don't want to get to the top. "Women tend to leave not just because of children or the family, but also because of an underlying dissatisfaction with the job," according to Freada Klein, president of a Cambridge consulting firm, quoted in one typical feature story about women who are "trying to fashion a broader meaning of success." *Fortune* itself reports that the business of helping women get off the fast-track is booming.

Richard Hokenson, chief economist at Donaldson, Lufkin & Jenrette, has earned the ire of many feminists by arguing that the slowdown in the growth rate of workforce participation by women aged twenty-five to thirty-four, and a decline in the participation rates of women twenty to twenty-four that began in the early 1990s reflect the fact that women who do have the choice today—the privileged few whose spouses earn enough to support the family—are choosing not to work. Among older women, those who have already begun the climb to the top, the trend even has a name: "Brenda Barnes syndrome," after the high-powered executive who made headlines when she traded in one of the most powerful corporate jobs in America to spend more time doing other things, including being with her family.

Whether Hokenson is right or not about this trend and what it represents, even a cursory survey of magazine covers and feature stories in recent years affirms the change in the atmosphere. So do countless interviews with ambitious women, who now find themselves on the defensive at cocktail parties, as perfect strangers grill them about their household arrangements. "You mean you really do mergers and acquisitions?" one female partner who does (one of the few) is regularly asked. "But what about your children?" The subtext is clear. Is she a bad mother? Does she ever see her children? Of course, no one ever asks these questions of men; they ask them about their deals.

The conventional wisdom is that young women today are even less ambitious than my generation was. Not confronting as much explicit discrimination, they make the mistake of not believing that it is there. Faced with doors that are half open instead of those that are slammed shut, they assume that the choices they are being offered are the only ones there could be.

Every year, I ask my students in gender discrimination how many of them expect to make partner in a major firm or become corporate counsel in the next ten years—the traditional "power" jobs in the law, the ones that come with the power to change the rules for others. Every year, fewer and fewer women raise their hands. Lately, I've had classes with none at all. Judge Patricia Wald of the United States Court of Appeals for the District of Columbia Circuit tells the story of showing the ABA report documenting the continued sexism in New York law firms to her female law clerks, who have to be the top graduates of the top law schools just to get that job. She expected them to react as she did: horrified at the continued discrimination, determined to do something about it. Instead, they dismissed the report with little more than a shrug. Who would want to work there anyway? So what if the people who do get those jobs end up running the world, wielding power not only as lawyers but as judges, politicians, advisers to presidents.

And who's to say they're wrong? I understand why young women look at what it takes to make partner, break through, climb the slippery pole, and decide they'd rather do car pool. I understand why Gina Occan is so unusual, destined to be unusual.

As it turned out, the University of Southern California offered me opportunities that Harvard did not; it was not a step down, in any sense. But even if it had been, I would not have regretted leaving Harvard. Hooray for Gina, but not for me.

Boys' rules. Boys' rules say that career matters more than family, that success is measured in partnerships and titles, that power is its own reward. And then, I would always say to great laughter, they end up at fifty, kids gone, careers at a dead-end, and we want to live like them?

There was a time in my life when I looked for glass ceilings to shatter. The *Harvard Law Review,* presidential politics, Harvard Law School—show me the challenge, and I would rise to it. I went back and forth between Harvard and Washington, and I moved very quickly. I lived as if work was all that mattered. Work was my escape, my source of satisfaction, my family. But I always knew what I wanted. When the time came to make a choice, for me, it was no choice. I knew I wanted children. "Knew" doesn't describe it. I have never been so certain of anything in my life. That's why I went to USC.

My friend Pam says that more and more women she talks to today are defining ambition in their own terms, setting ambitious goals but not necessarily the ones men would, going back to school at fifty, learning to ride horses, becoming high school teachers. More power to them.

But most of the women I know who are switching careers have run into a cement wall in the one they were in. Most of the women I know going back to school at fifty do so after realizing that it's impossible to get the kind of job they'd want, the kind that would challenge them. Most of the ones horseback riding would welcome some other challenges in their lives.

In one way or another, they put aside their ambitions for their families, just as a younger generation is doing now, just as many baby-boom careerists did in their forties. They did so and discovered that the rules of the public world were not structured for people who follow that path; that a price, sometimes a very large price, must be paid.

I have always thought of myself as an ambitious woman, and no one has ever disagreed. I am ambitious, as women go. I am not embarrassed to say that I like power. But I have not been as ambitious as I might have been; I have not always maximized my power. And it isn't just my family that has stood in the way of that. At critical points in my career, I have let other values stand in the way of my pursuit of power, making decisions that few men I know would have.

I did not put Michael Dukakis in a tank—the infamous shot that came to symbolize that losing campaign. I wanted him to be at a school. Guns or butter. It didn't matter. The truth was that he had stopped listening to me months before; the last piece of advice I gave him that he followed was to select Lloyd Bentsen as his running mate. Throughout the long, hot summer of 1988, I kept the machinery of a presidential campaign going, but I barely talked to the candidate whose campaign I was supposed to be running.

I also kept my mouth shut. I never talked or wrote about it, until now, twelve years later, when it is a story about me, not him. I agonized, though, and I have second-guessed myself many times. The poll numbers were dropping. Bush was out there hitting hard. The consultants I wanted Dukakis didn't, the ones we did have got less time with him than I got, and I had the candidate scolding me for daring to interrupt him when he was interviewing judges for superior court appointments.

I am pretty sure I know what most men would have done; I have watched men in that position carefully in the years since. They would have protected themselves. Leaked the truth to the press. Written a cover memo of all the advice they'd given that hadn't been taken and given it to a few carefully selected reporters. I would never do such things because I thought they would be disloyal. I would be putting myself first, putting my survival in front of the candidate's. I thought that was wrong.

But here's the irony: It might have been better if I had. It would certainly have been better for me. I wouldn't have taken as much heat as I did. And it might also have gotten Dukakis out of the state house and onto the road. The boys leak to protect themselves, but that isn't their only rationale. One way you communicate with a candidate who is refusing to listen to anyone is by having him read the advice in the paper. It infuriates them, creates conflict and explosions. It is hardball, and if you lose, you're dead. But it gets their attention. Was I afraid to do it? Why didn't I call in some Washington big shots, sound the alarm? Selfless, or scared?

As it was, his numbers kept dropping, and on Labor Day, I stood by graciously and welcomed back the man I had replaced, with relief that maybe he could manage the candidate, and anger that what could have been handled with some sensitivity to me, wasn't. The candidate didn't call.

I started doing talk radio a year later at KABC in Los Angeles, then the biggest talk radio station in town. I loved it. If I do say so myself (and being a woman, this isn't easy), I was very good at it, and the more of it I did, the better I got. When I started, Michael Jackson (not the singer) was the dean of talk radio in Los Angeles. For more than two decades, he had been talking from 9 A.M. to 1 P.M. every day at KABC. He was an institution. He had never had a permanent substitute. When he went on vacation, they used revolving hosts, until I came along. I sat in for him whenever he went on vacation (four weeks every year) or took a day off or got sick; I sat in for three months when he had open heart surgery. I also had my own show, every Saturday and Sunday from 10 A.M. to 1 P.M.

I'd been doing this for about four years when station management approached me one day, in the strictest confidence. They wanted to give me Michael's job. His ratings were falling, his contract negotiations had collapsed, his contract would expire in a matter of days, and they wanted a signed deal with me by the time it did. Then he'd come to work on Friday, and they'd tell him he was finished. I could tell no one. This is how it's done in radio. Who should they call to work out the details? What was my lawyer's name?

It would have been a great job. I wanted it. I thought I could do it. I'd assumed, for the past year or so, that the job would be mine someday, in a year or five, when Michael retired, or was eased out. I had all kinds of ideas of how I would give new life to the show, bring in more female listeners, take on Rush Limbaugh. And if I could do it in Los Angeles, what next?

But I couldn't do it this way. It would be wrong. It was too mean. I had sat in for this man when he was sick. He trusted me to be his permanent replacement. I told my lawyer that I was going to call Michael. He thought I was out of my mind. He told me I was giving up one of the best jobs in radio, that if Michael knew they had offered it to me, he would immediately come in and accept whatever their last offer had been. I understood that. I called anyway. His wife got on the other line. It was a very emotional conversation. They thanked me over and over. I had saved him. What a wonderful person I was. What a girl.

Michael's ratings kept dropping. New management came in and started bringing in more and more right-wing hosts. I knew that if and when Michael left or was pushed out, the chances of my replacing him now were small to none, but they left me alone on Saturdays and Sundays, and I convinced myself that was plenty.

I was sitting at my desk working one morning when Judith Michaelson, the radio reporter for the *Los Angeles Times,* called. She had just heard Michael say on the radio that he was being replaced in the Monday through Friday slot, but would henceforth be heard on Saturday and Sunday from 10 A.M. to 1 P.M. Who was replacing him Monday through Friday? Wasn't that my weekend slot he was taking? I told her the truth: I had no idea what she was talking about. She was mortified that she was the one to tell me. Neither of us could believe it. I could believe that the new management had some right-winger waiting in the wings to take over for Michael (they did), but I couldn't believe that he'd take my slot as a consolation prize (in fact, he'd insisted on it) without even having the decency to call me the night before. But of course, that's how it's done in radio.

Getting power and holding on to it by the rules of today's workplace is not often, maybe not ever, a contest of niceness. Modern-day Machiavellis are more often feared than loved, which runs counter to my instincts, and those of many women. If America's most powerful women are of at least two minds about their power, reluctant even to admit that they have it, much less that they like it, should it surprise anyone that the rest of us are unwilling to do what it takes to get it? If nice guys finish last, should it shock us when nice girls don't even get in the game?

The reason Richard Hokenson's drop-out theory is unpopular with feminists is not because it is necessarily wrong but because of its potential impact on the overwhelming majority of women who are still working. The reason Brenda Barnes's resignation generated so much ire among corporate women is not because she was wrong in the way she balanced her life, but because of the fear that other women would pay for it. The perception, if not the reality, that women drop off the fast-track at higher rates than men makes it easier to justify the failure to accommodate and promote the ones who stay.

Behind closed doors, consultant Freada Klein has no doubt that executives are already saying just that; she has heard it. "Senior managers say, 'We are spending too much money training women, and it isn't worth it.' " Some women say the same thing. "I cannot see how we can argue for equal numbers of women in medical school or law school or plumbing school, if they start dropping out," argues Joan K. Peters, author of *When Mothers Work: Loving Our Children Without Sacrificing Ourselves.* "It is a contradiction."

Most of us are accustomed to thinking of those women who drop out to spend time with their children or pull back to avoid stepping on toes as acting selflessly. That is certainly how I felt when I turned down the best job in radio. It is how I felt when I accepted responsibility for decisions I didn't make in the Dukakis campaign. Putting yourself first feels selfish, which is one of the reasons we find it so hard to do, one of the reasons that Gina Occan's decision to move to Cambridge with her baby so she could attend Harvard ultimately raised questions even for me, one of her strongest supporters.

But dropping out, pulling back, letting niceness get the best of you, not asking for enough, not pushing hard enough, is also a selfish decision, from the collective perspective of feminism. It negatively affects other women. It retards change. There are occasions when the unselfish act is not to settle for less and convince ourselves that we are better for it, but to demand more, and use what we get to improve the lot of others.

When I was on the radio, so were more women—as guests, producers, and callers. There were very few women in prime-time radio, in Los Angeles or anywhere, then or now. I was not the only one who paid the price of my niceness to Michael Jackson; so did women who were looking for the sort of voice in the public world that I would have given them. If I'd thought about that at the time, I might well have made a different decision. I wish I had.

In his wonderfully named and wonderfully readable book, *Why Is Sex Fun,* Jared Diamond explains why it is that men don't breast-feed, and why women don't know when they ovulate. In every species in which embryos or offspring require the care of at least one parent, there is a battle of the sexes as to who will provide it. Professor Diamond explains that three factors determine who will take care of the off-spring, and who will desert or play the secondary role: the relative size of the mother's and father's investments in the embryo, the other opportunities for reproduction foreclosed by childcare, and the certainty of maternity or paternity. Human mothers invest not only nine months in pregnancy, but in the hunter-gatherer days, up to four years in lactation, during which a woman is much less likely to reproduce. Men are immediately available to reproduce again. No tests are required to be certain of who the mother is, while males who devoted themselves to childcare might find themselves tending to the genes of another man. All of these factors tend to make a father more likely to desert than a mother. In the case of humans, who require secondary care as well, what keeps the men around in evolutionary terms is the fact that ovulation is unknown, and therefore a man can't be certain that he has successfully inseminated the woman, or that another man won't come along and do so if he leaves prematurely.

What evolutionary biology suggests, what three decades of law reform underscore, what the numbers tell us, what each of us knows is that the incorporation of women into the public world, the best use of all of our talents, requires more than opening doors. It's not a pipeline issue. How could it be, in a world structured by and for the winners of the game of child-rearing chicken?

We have begun that process here and there, with family leave and maternity leave required by law, with Catalyst awards and on-site childcare. It is further along in some work-places than others. But it goes beyond family-friendliness. The treatment of extraordinary women, the fact that even the Hillarys and Ginas are treated differently, is a test not of the structure of the workplace but its ideology. It is a measure of how women are considered.

We could take it on, all of it. We could start counting and demand results, from the inside and the outside; we could run for office and support one another; we could use our buying power and our voting strength to reward good behavior and punish bad. The question women, particularly middle-class women in America who have power, face is whether we (still) have the ambition to change things. It is a special kind of ambition, an ambition for something larger than one's own success.

I have all that I want, my girlfriends who are, like me, old enough to find ourselves surrounded by cancer, tell one another. But mortality carries with it more than one lesson. To enjoy life, yes; but also to make a difference.

The gift that feminism gave to me as a young woman was a reason to stand up for myself, a mission that was larger than myself, and a community with whom I shared that mission. It was the gift that brought me success at Harvard Law School, an environment incredibly hostile to women in many ways, not the least of which was the self-fulfilling prophecy that women couldn't and wouldn't do very well. I saw myself as carrying a mantle, and so did my friends. Once I got those two A+'s my first semester, I was positioned to break through, and they were going to do everything they could to help me. When I was tired and depressed, they fed me and made me laugh. When the managing editor called me an ambitious chick, they helped me find the poster that said "Women are not chicks." By the spring, when people put their names in to be considered for the job of president of the *Harvard Law Review,* it was assumed, by me and everyone else, that I'd be a leading candidate. It was a goal that would never have occurred to a girl who took it for granted that men were presidents and women were first ladies. But I wasn't a girl who accepted traditions anymore; I was a feminist with a point to make.

I don't think I could have done it without my friends, and all they meant to me. Or rather, I wouldn't have done it. The work I did myself; in that sense, I certainly could have done it. And I was very lucky to find myself in an institution that prided itself on its merit system. But what kept me up at 2 A.M. was the idea that I was part of a larger effort, that I was doing this to prove something bigger than myself. I did very well at Wellesley, but I didn't feel any need to run the student government, to edit the school newspaper, to be elected class president. Harvard did that to me. Harvard and feminism.

There will be a lot of girls trying out for little league, I assured my daughter last spring. There were not a lot of girls. My daughter was the only girl on her team; some of the teams didn't have any girls. We were both disappointed.

As the only girl on her team, I think my daughter felt a special responsibility. She was determined to succeed (or at least not be the worst), to show that a girl could do it. When she was frustrated and felt like a failure, she had something to hold on to. She had a mission, and she fulfilled it.

The name of that mission is feminism. Its gift is the idea that a girl can be whoever she wants, that she too can grow up to be president. Its gift is the faith that both my children—my daughter and my son—can be free to be their best selves. But with the gift comes the responsibility to fulfill its promise, to stand up as a woman, if not for your own sake, then for the sake of those who come next.

We stand for the day when we don't have to.

For me, and I hope for my daughter, feminism is a lesson in the possibilities of being a truly autonomous person. I teach

it, and try to live it, as a critical perspective that opens up possibilities, not one that shuts them down and turns viewers into
victims. See the unfairness, the discrimination, the line-
drawing, the status quo, as what it is; see it so you are not
bound by it. Understand that you are not alone, that it is not
you, that this is bigger and beyond you. Understand those
things not so that you will be paralyzed, but so that you will
have the strength to act. Know that the law is on your side and
that much of what was once considered acceptable no longer
is; understand that revolution is possible, that we have already
changed the world, and all we have to do is finish the job.

Bibliography

CHAPTER ONE: IN THE MIDDLE OF A REVOLUTION

Bradwell v. Illinois, 83 U.S. (16 Wall.) 130, 21 L.Ed. 442 (1872).

"The Budget Deal: Compromise at Last." *New York Times,* October 16, 1998.

"The Budget Deal: Details and Dollars." *New York Times,* October 16, 1998.

Cott, Nancy. *The Grounding of Modern Feminism.* New Haven: Yale University Press, 1987.

Dinnerstein, Dorothy. *The Mermaid and the Minotaur: Sexual Arrangements and Human Malaise.* New York: Harper & Row, 1976.

Epstein, Cynthia Fuchs. *Deceptive Distinctions: Sex, Gender, and the Social Order.* New Haven: Yale University Press, 1988.

————. *Women in Law.* Urbana: University of Illinois Press, 1993.

Epstein, Richard. "Two Challenges for Feminist Thought." *Harvard Journal of Law and Public Policy* 18 (1995): 331.

Faludi, Susan. *Backlash: The Undeclared War Against American Women.* New York: Crown, 1991.

Folpe, Jane M., Deirdre P. Lanning, and Tyler Maroney. *"Fortune's* 50 Most Powerful Women." *Fortune,* October 25, 1999.

Goodman, Ellen. "Somebody Is Getting Lost in Hillary-for-Senate Campaign." *The Dallas Morning News* Viewpoints, March 26, 2000.

————. *Turning Points.* Garden City, NY: Doubleday, 1979.

Interview with feminist Camille Paglia. Fox News Network's "The Edge with Paula Zahn," April 18, 2000.

Jaggar, Alison. "On Sexual Equality." *Ethics* 84 (July 1974): 275.

Kaminer, Wendy. "Feminism's Identity Crisis." *The Atlantic,* October 1993.

————. "Feminism's Third Wave: What Do Young Women Want?" *New York Times Book Review,* June 4, 1995.

————. "Will Class Trump Gender? The New Assault on Feminism." *The American Prospect* 29 (November–December 1996).

Mill, John Stuart, and Harriet Taylor Mill. *Essays on Sex Equality.* Edited by Alice S. Rossi. Chicago: University of Chicago Press, 1970.

Rhode, Deborah. *Speaking of Sex: The Denial of Gender Equality.* Cambridge, MA: Harvard University Press, 1997.

Rivers, Caryl. *More Joy Than Rage: Crossing Generations with the New Feminism.* Hanover, NH: University Press of New England, 1991.

Sommers, Christina Hoff. *Who Stole Feminism? How Women Have Betrayed Women.* New York: Simon & Schuster, 1994.

Tobias, Sheila. *Faces of Feminism: An Activist's Reflection on the Women's Movement.* Boulder, CO: Westview Press, 1997.

Wasserstrom, Richard. "Racism and Sexism." In *Philosophy and Social Issues: Five Studies.* Notre Dame: University of Notre Dame Press, 1980.

Williams, Joan. *Unbending Gender: Why Family and Work Conflict and What to Do About It.* New York: Oxford University Press, 2000.

Young, Cathy. "Speaking of Sex: The Denial of Gender Inequality." *Reason* Book Review, April 1998.

NOTE: There are many issues that I don't make any claim to addressing in this book. The intersections of sex and race, and sex and sexual orientation, raise issues that cannot be dealt with in a shorthand way, and while some of the questions raised are similar to those addressed here, the more important point is that many are not. If Professor Kimberle Crenshaw is right that the most privileged subgroup within a discriminated-against group tends to fare best—heterosexual, white, middle-class women being her prime example—then it is significant that this subgroup has not indeed fared as well as might be expected and is not in the position to help the less privileged as much as many of us would expect they should. There is a growing literature on issues of race and sex, and lesbian feminism. See, for example, bell hooks, *Ain't I a Woman: Black Women and Feminism* (Boston: South End Press, 1981); Patricia Hill Collins, *Black Feminist Thought: Knowledge, Consciousness, and the Politics of Empowerment* (Boston: Unwin Hyman, 1990); Kimberle Crenshaw, "Demarginalizing the

Intersection of Race and Sex: A Black Feminist Critique of Antidiscrimination Doctrine, Feminist Theory and Antiracist Policies," in *University of Chicago Legal Forum* 139 (1989); Kimberle Crenshaw, "Race, Gender and Sexual Harassment," in *Southern California Law Review* 65 (1992): 1467; Adrienne Rich, "Compulsory Heterosexuality and Lesbian Existence," in *Signs* 5 (1980): 631; and Patricia Cain, "Feminist Jurisprudence: Grounding the Theories," in *Berkeley Women's Law Journal* 4 (1989): 191.

CHAPTER TWO:
ON BEING EXTRAORDINARY

Calvo, Dana. "Female Anchors on Local TV Paid 28 Percent Less." *Los Angeles Times,* June 1, 2000.

Catalyst. "The 1998 Catalyst Census of Women Corporate Officers and Top Earners of the *Fortune* 500," 1999.

Dalton, Dan, and Catherine Daily. "Women in the Boardroom Are Still on the Outside." *Chicago Tribune,* March 14, 1999.

Drell, Adrienne. "Making the Case for Women." *Chicago Sun-Times,* March 25, 1998.

Ezold v. Wolf, Block, Schorr and Solis-Cohen, 983 F.2d 509 (3d Cir. 1993).

Hansell, Saul. "Time Warner and AOL Offer a Blueprint." *New York Times,* May 5, 2000.

Lancaster, Hal. "Women at Kraft Tell How to Be Big Cheese While Handling Family." *Wall Street Journal,* April 23, 1996.

Layne, Peggy. "Women in Engineering: How Far Have They Come?" *Chemical Engineering* 105 (1998): 84.

Massachusetts Institute of Technology. "A Study on the Status of Women Faculty in Science at MIT," 1999.

Morris, Betsy. "Executive Women Confront Midlife Crisis." *Fortune,* September 18, 1995.

Robinson-Jacobs, Karen. "When It Comes to Pay, It's Still a Man's World." *Los Angeles Times,* April 23, 1998.

Rosener, Judy B. *America's Competitive Secret: Utilizing Women as a Management Strategy.* New York: Oxford University Press, 1995.

Shellenberger, Sue. "Women's Resignation from Top Pepsi Post Rekindles Debate." *Wall Street Journal,* October 8, 1997.

Solomon, Charlene Marmer. "Women Are Still Undervalued: Bridge the Parity Gap." *Workforce,* May 1998.

Wellington, Sheila M., and E. James Brennan. "The Pay Gap for Women Persists." *Wall Street Journal* Letters to the Editor, September 2, 1998.

White, Joseph B., and Carol Hymowitz. "Broken Glass: Watershed Generation of Women Executives Is Rising to the Top." *Wall Street Journal,* February 10, 1997.

CHAPTER THREE: EQUAL UNDER THE LAW

Bradwell v. Illinois, 83 U.S. (16 Wall.) 130, 21 L.Ed. 442 (1872).

California Federal Savings & Loan Association v. Guerra, 479 U.S. 272, 93 L.Ed.2d 613, 107 S.Ct. 683 (1987).

Ely, John Hart. *Democracy and Distrust: A Theory of Judicial Review.* Cambridge, MA: Harvard University Press, 1980.

Fineman, Martha Albert. "Feminist Theory in Law: The Difference it Makes." *Columbia Journal of Gender and Law* 2 (1992): 1.

Finley, Lucinda. "Transcending Equality Theory: A Way Out of the Maternity and the Workplace Debate." *Columbia Law Review* 86 (1986): 1118.

Fiss, Owen. "What Is Feminism?" *Arizona State Law Journal* 26 (1994): 413.

Frontiero v. Richardson, 411 U.S. 677, 93 S.Ct. 1764, 36 L.Ed.2d 583 (1973).

Ginsburg, Ruth Bader. "Gender and the Constitution." *University of Cincinnati Law Review* 44 (1975): 1.

Goesaert v. Cleary, 335 U.S. 464, 69 S.Ct. 198, 93 L.Ed. 163 (1948).

Hoyt v. Florida, 368 U.S. 57, 82 S.Ct. 159, 7 L.Ed.2d 118 (1961).

Kay, Herma Hill, and Martha S. West. *Text, Cases and Materials on Sex-Based Discrimination.* 4th ed. St. Paul, MN: West, 1996.

MacKinnon, Catharine A. *Sexual Harassment of Working Women: A Case of Sex Discrimination.* New Haven: Yale University Press, 1979.

Minow, Martha. *Not Only for Myself: Identity, Politics, and the Law.* New York: New Press, 1997.

Muller v. Oregon, 208 U.S. 412, 28 S.Ct. 324, 52 L.Ed. 551 (1908).

Radin, Margaret. "The Pragmatist and the Feminist." *Southern California Law Review* 63 (1990): 1699.

Reed v. Reed, 404 U.S. 71, 92 S.Ct. 251, 30 L.Ed.2d 225 (1971).

Rhode, Deborah. *Justice and Gender: Sex Discrimination and the Law.* Cambridge, MA: Harvard University Press, 1989.

Siegel, Reva B. "Employment Equality Under the Pregnancy Discrimination Act of 1978." *Yale Law Journal* 94 (1985): 929.

Weinberger v. Wiesenfeld, 420 U.S. 636, 43 L.Ed.2d 514, 95 S.Ct. 1225 (1975).

CHAPTER FOUR: THE FACTS OF LIFE

Abramson, Jill, and Barbara Franklin. *Where They Are Now: The Story of the Women of Harvard Law 1974*. Garden City, NY: Doubleday, 1986.

American Bar Association. "Unfinished Business: Overcoming the Sisyphus Factor: A Report on the Status of Women in the Legal Profession," December 1995.

Bates, James. "Older Writers Put Out to Pasture in Hollywood." *Los Angeles Times,* October 27, 1998.

Bernstein, Nina. "Equal Opportunity Recedes for Most Female Lawyers." *New York Times,* January 8, 1996.

Bilimoria, Diana, and Sandy Kristin Piderit. "Board Committee Memberships: Effects of Sex-Based Bias." *Academy of Management Journal* 37 (1994): 1453.

Catalyst. "Catalyst Census Finds 86 Percent of *Fortune* 500 Companies Have Women Directors," October 15, 1998.

————. "Census Spotlight Now Shines on 1000," February 2000.

————. "The 1998 Catalyst Census of Women Corporate Officers and Top Earners of the *Fortune* 500," 1999.

————. "Women Break the 10 Percent Barrier in *Fortune* 500 Boardrooms; But Represent Less," December 11, 1996.

————. "Women of Color Report a 'Concrete Ceiling' Barring Their Advancement in Corporate America," July 13, 1999.

Center for the American Woman and Politics. "Fact Sheets: Women Candidates 1998 Summary: Women in Elective Office," 1998.

Collins, Gail. "A Social Glacier Roars." *New York Times Magazine,* May 16, 1999.

Costello, Cynthia B., Shari Miles, and Anne J. Stone, eds. *The American Woman 1999–2000: A Century of Change—What's Next?* New York: Norton, 1998.

Council on Graduate Medical Education. "Women and Medicine," July 1995.

Cox, T. H., and C. Harquail. "Career Paths and Career Success in the Early Career Stages of Male and Female MBAs." *Journal of Vocational Behavior* 39 (1991).

Dalton, Dan, and Catherine Daily. "Women in the Boardroom Are Still on the Outside." *Chicago Tribune,* March 14, 1999.

DeGeorge, Gail. "Where Are They Now? *Business Week*'s Leading Corporate Women of 1976." *Business Week,* June 22, 1987.

Epstein, Cynthia Fuchs, et al. "Glass Ceilings and Open Doors: Women's Advancement in the Legal Profession." Report to the Bar Association of the City of New York, 1995. In *Fordham Law Review* 64 (1995): 291.

Federal Glass Ceiling Commission. "Good for Business: Making Full Use of the Nation's Human Capital," 1995.

Folpe, Jane M., Deirdre P. Lanning, and Tyler Maroney. "*Fortune*'s 50 Most Powerful Women." *Fortune,* October 25, 1999.

Foster, S. Elizabeth. "The Glass Ceiling in the Legal Profession." *UCLA Law Review* 42 (1995): 1631.

France, Mike. "In-House Counsel Pay Shows Gender Gap." *National Law Journal,* November 28, 1994.

Fuchs, Victor. *Women's Quest for Economic Equality.* Cambridge, MA: Harvard University Press, 1988.

Hansell, Saul. "Time Warner and AOL Offer a Blueprint." *New York Times,* May 5, 2000.

Huang, Wynn R. "Gender Differences in the Earnings of Lawyers." *Columbia Journal of Law and Social Problems* 30 (1997): 267.

McNamara, Joseph D. "Breaking the Glass Shield for Women." *Los Angeles Times,* May 16, 1999.

Marks, Janet R., Mary Kay Dugan, and Betsy Payn. "Why Women Drop Out of Graduate Management Education: Answers from the GMAC Data." *Graduate Management Admission Council 1997 Selections,* Autumn 1997.

Mills, C. Wright. *The Power Elite.* New York: Oxford University Press, 1956.

National Bureau of Economic Research. "Career and Family: College Women Look to the Past," July 1995.

National Committee on Pay Equity. "Women, Family and Future Trends: A Selected Research Overview," December 1998.

"The Players." *Worth Magazine,* November 1998.

"Reality Check." *Hollywood Reporter,* December 1, 1998.

Robertson, Wyndham. "The Top Women in Big Business." *Fortune,* July 17, 1978.

Robinson, J. G., and J. S. McIlwee. "Women in Engineering: A Promise Unfulfilled?" *Social Problems* 36 (April 1998): 455.

Schneider, Alison. "Why Don't Women Publish as Much as Men?" *The Chronicle of Higher Education,* September 11, 1998.

Shultz, Vicki. "Telling Stories About Women and Work." *Harvard Law Review* 103 (1990): 1749.

Tripoli, Lori. "More Than You Think, Not as Many as You'd Hope." *Of Counsel,* May 4, 1998.

Valian, Virginia. *Why So Slow?: The Advancement of Women.* Cambridge, MA: MIT Press, 1998.

Wald, Patricia M. "Glass Ceilings and Open Doors: A Reaction." *Fordham Law Review* 65 (1996): 603.

Wellington, Sheila. "Women on Corporate Boards: The Challenge of Change." *Directorship Newsletter,* December 1994.

Wellington, Sheila M., and E. James Brennan. "The Pay Gap for Women Persists." *Wall Street Journal* Letters to the Editor, September 2, 1998.

Wilkens, David, and G. Mita Gulati. "Why Are There So Few Black Lawyers in Corporate Law Firms? An Institutional Analysis." *California Law Review* 84 (1996): 493.

Williams, Christine L. *Still a Man's World: Men Who Do "Women's Work."* Berkeley: University of California Press, 1995.

Wise, Daniel. "City Bar Spearheads Efforts to Promote Women." *New York Law Journal,* April 8, 1998. (Similar efforts have been underway since I was in law school. At the firms in New York with the best records of promoting women, two out of three of the new partners are men; at the firms with the worst records, it's nine out ot ten, on average, or even ten out of ten.)

Zweigenhaft, Richard, and G. William Domhoff. *Diversity in the Power Elite: Have Women and Minorities Reached the Top?* New Haven: Yale University Press, 1998.

CHAPTER FIVE:
MOTHERHOOD AS DESTINY

Abrams, Kathryn. "Gender Discrimination and the Transformation of Workplace Norms." *Vanderbilt Law Review* 42 (1989): 1183.

Alter, Jonathan. "It's 4:00 P.M. Do You Know Where Your Children Are?" *Newsweek,* April 27, 1998.

Armour, Stephanie. "On the Clock: Working Parents Take Issue." *USA Today,* May 27, 1999.

Bipartisan Commission on Family and Medical Leave. Report. Summer 1995.

Blau, Francine, and Ronald Ehrenburg, eds. *Gender and Family Issues in the Workplace.* New York: R. Sage Foundation, 1997.

Chira, Susan. *A Mother's Place: Taking the Debate About Working Mothers Beyond Guilt and Blame.* New York: HarperCollins, 1998.

Crittenden, Danielle. *What Our Mothers Didn't Tell Us: Why Happiness Eludes the Modern Woman.* New York: Simon & Schuster, 1999.

Fuchs, Victor, *Women's Quest for Economic Equality.* Cambridge, MA: Harvard University Press, 1988.

Griggs v. Duke Power Co., 401 U.S. 424 (1971).

Hicks, Lynn. "Derailing the Mommy Track." *The Des Moines Register,* April 13, 1998.

Hochschild, Arlie, and Anne Machung. *The Second Shift: Working Parents and the Revolution at Home.* New York: Viking, 1989.

Jacobs, Deborah. "Exiting the 'Mommy Track.'" *Chicago Tribune,* January 1, 1995.

Korzec, Rebecca. "Working on the Mommy-Track: Motherhood and Women Lawyers." *Hastings Women's Law Journal* 8 (1997): 117.

McCaffrey, Edward J. "Equality of the Right Sort," *UCLA Women's Law Journal* 6 (1996): 289.

McGinnis, John O. "Strong, Silent, Redundant." *Wall Street Journal* Book Review, May 27, 1999.

"Mothers Can't Win." *New York Times Magazine* Special Issue, April 5, 1998.

National Foundation for Women Business Owners. "Access to Credit to Improve for Women Business Owners," November 17, 1998.

———. "Characteristics of Women Entrepreneurs Worldwide Are Revealed," March 5, 1999.

———. "Entrepreneurial Ideas Motivate Women to Start Businesses," February 24, 1998.

———. "First Selection of Leading Women Entrepreneurs Worldwide," April 14, 1997.

———. "Home-Based Women-Owned Businesses Number and Employ Millions," November 16, 1995.

———. "New Study Quantifies Thinking and Management Style Difference Between Women and Men Business Owners," July 19, 1994.

———. "Technology Key to Growth and Success of Women-Owned Businesses," April 26, 1995.

———. "Venture Capital: Next Frontier for Women Entrepreneurs," March 25, 1999.

———. "Women Business Owners' Economic Impact Re-Affirmed," March 27, 1996.

———. "Women Business Owners Give Priority to Retirement Plans," November 13, 1997.

———. "Women Entrepreneurs Embrace the Internet and Information Technology," September 30, 1997.

———. "Women-Owned Businesses Top 9 Million in 1999," May 11, 1999.

———. "Women-Owned Firms Are Selling to Governments, Corporations," October 15, 1998.

———. "Women-Owned Firms Increase in 50 Metro Areas," March 26, 1997.

Pacific Research Institute. "Free Markets, Free Choices: Women in the Workforce," December 1995.

Pasternak, Judy. "Opting for the Job of Mothering." *Los Angeles Times,* December 12, 1997.

Peterson, Karen S. "Dads Less Flexible in Child Care Crises," *USA Today,* July 8, 1997.

Schor, Juliet. *The Overworked American: The Unexpected Decline of Leisure.* New York: Basic Books, 1991.

Schwartz, Felice. "Management Women and the New Facts of Life." *Harvard Business Review* 67 (1989): 65.

Shellenbarger, Sue. "The New Pace of Work Makes Taking a Break for Child Care Scarier." *Wall Street Journal,* May 19, 1999. (Shellenbarger writes smart columns every week about the conflicts between work and family; it is the only such column I have found, outside the "Living/Style" pages in any major newspaper. By placing it on the front page of the second section, the *Journal* seems to recognize that balancing is an economic issue as well as a lifestyle question.)

Smolowe, Jill. "The Stalled Revolution." *Time,* May 6, 1996.

Tavris, Carol. "Goodbye to Momism," *New York Times Book Review,* May 3, 1998.

Vogel, Susan. "Babies and Briefs: Rhetoric Yields to Reality." *Legal Times,* January 23, 1995.

Weinstein, Michael M. "Economic Scene." *New York Times,* May 27, 1999.

Wood, Robert G., Mary E. Corcoran, and Paul N. Courant. "Pay Differences Among the Highly Paid: The Male-Female Earnings Gap in Lawyers' Salaries." *Journal of Labor Economics* 11 (1993): 417.

CHAPTER SIX: THE COMFORT FACTOR

Boverman, I. K., S. R. Vogel, D. M. Broverman, F. E. Clarkson, and P. S. Rosenkrantz. "Sex Role Stereotypes: A Current Appraisal." *Journal of Social Issues* 28, no. 2 (1972).

Chamallas, Martha. "Structuralist and Cultural Domination Theories Meet Title VII: Some Contemporary Influences." *Michigan Law Review* 92 (1994): 2370.

Chambers, Marcia. *The Unplayable Lie: The Untold Story of Women and Discrimination in American Golf.* New York: Pocket Books, 1995.

Deaux, K. "From Individual Differences to Social Categories: Analysis of a Decade's Research on Gender." *American Psychologist* 39 (1984).

———. "Sex and Gender." *Annual Review of Psychology* 36 (1985).

Driscoll, Dawn-Marie, and Carol R. Goldberg. *Members of the Club: The Coming of Age of Executive Women.* New York: Free Press, 1993.

Frenier, Carol. *Business and the Feminine Principle: The Untapped Resource.* Boston: Butterworth-Heinemann, 1997.

Gibb-Clark, Margaret. "Female Executives, Male CEOs Differ on What Blocks Women from the Top Chair, Study Finds." *The Globe and Mail* (Toronto), December 10, 1997.

Guinier, Lani, et al. "Becoming Gentlemen: Women's Experiences at One Ivy League Law School." *University of Pennsylvania Law Review* 143 (1994).

Harrington, Mona. *Women Lawyers: Rewriting the Rules.* New York: Knopf, 1993.

Horner, Matina. "Toward an Understanding of Achievement-Related Conflicts in Women." *Journal of Social Issues* 28 (1972): 57.

Kanter, Rosabeth Moss. *Men and Women of the Corporation.* New York: Basic Books, 1993.

Maccoby, E. E., and C. N. Jacklin. *The Psychology of Sex Differences.* Stanford: Stanford University Press, 1974.

Menkel-Meadow, Carrie. "Exploring a Research Agenda on the Feminization of the Legal Profession." *Law and Social Inquiry* 14 (1989): 289.

Morrison, Ann M., Randall P. White, and Ellen Van Velsor. *Breaking the Glass Ceiling: Can Women Reach the Top of America's Largest Corporations?* Reading, MA: Addison-Wesley, 1992.

Oldenburg, Don. "Women at the Top: Beyond the Glass Ceiling." *Washington Post,* August 1, 1995.

Powell, Gary. *Women and Men in Management.* Newbury Park, CA: Sage, 1988.

Price Waterhouse v. Hopkins, 490 U.S. 228 (1990).

Rosener, Judy. "Ways Women Lead." *Harvard Business Review,* December 1990.

CHAPTER SEVEN:
CHANGING THE FACE OF
CORPORATE AMERICA

Bilimoria, Diana, and Sandy Kristen Piderit. "Board Committee Memberships: Effects of Sex-Based Bias." *Academy of Management Journal* 37 (1994): 1453.

Catalyst. "Advancing Women in Business—The Catalyst Guide," 1998.

———. "1999 Catalyst Census of Women Board Directors of the *Fortune* 1000," 1999.

Chambliss, Elizabeth. "Organization Determinants of Law Firm Integration." *American University Law Review* 46 (February 1997): 669.

Francis, Mary. "Making Women Welcome: Lincoln National Among Best Firms for Women Execs." *The Indianapolis Star,* August 30, 1998.

Gasparino, Charles, and Randall Smith. "U.S. Agency Calls Morgan Stanley Biased Against Female Executive." *Wall Street Journal,* June 6, 2000.

Ghiloni, Beth W. "The Velvet Ghetto: Women, Power, and the Corporation." In *Power Elites and Organizations,* edited by G. William Domhoff and Thomas R. Dye. Newbury Park, CA: Sage, 1987.

Groves, Martha. "Some Firms Look Through Glass Ceiling to See Ways of Tapping Women's Talent." *Los Angeles Times,* July 12, 1998.

Jamieson, Kathleen Hall. *Beyond the Double Bind: Women and Leadership.* New York: Oxford University Press, 1995.

Kanter, Rosabeth Moss. *Men and Women of the Corporation.* New York: Basic Books, 1993.

Pappano, Laura. "Breaking Through." *Boston Magazine,* July 1993.

Pappas, Ben. "On My Mind: What's Worrying Top Executives." *Forbes,* May 5, 1997.

Plevans, Bettina. "Law Firms Partnership and Benefits Report," February 1998.

Rubin, Harriet. *The Princessa: Machiavelli for Women.* New York: Doubleday, 1997.

Schafran, Lynn Hecht. "Will Inquiry Produce Action? Studying the Effects of Gender in the Federal Courts." *University of Richmond Law Review* 32 (1998): 615.

"Why Law Firms Cannot Afford to Maintain the Mommy Track." *Harvard Law Review* 109 (1996): 1375, note.

Zweigenhaft, Richard, and G. William Domhoff. *Diversity in the Power Elite: Have Women and Minorities Reached the Top?* New Haven: Yale University Press, 1998.

CHAPTER EIGHT: SEXUAL POWER

Amiel, Barbara. "Feminism: What NOW?" *Wall Street Journal,* March 20, 1998.

Bernstein, Anita. "Treating Sexual Harassment with Respect." *Harvard Law Review* 111 (1997): 446.

Bryden, David, and Sonja Lengnick. "Rape in the Criminal Justice System." *Journal of Criminal Law and Criminology* 87 (1997): 1194.

Ceol, Dawn. "Thomas Denounces Lynching; Senators Question Nominee, Accuser." *Washington Times,* October 12, 1991.

Commonwealth v. Berkowitz, 641 A.2d 1161 (Pa. 1994).

Commonwealth v. Stockhammer, 570 N.E.2d 992 (1991).

Dripps, Donald. "Beyond Rape." *Columbia Law Review* 92 (1992): 1780.

Ehrenreich, Nancy. "Pluralist Myths and Powerless Men: The Ideology of Reasonableness in Sexual Harassment Law." *Yale Law Journal* 99 (1990): 1177.

Epstein, Cynthia Fuchs, et al. "Glass Ceilings and Open Doors: Women's Advancement in the Legal Profession." Report to the Bar Association of the City of New York, 1995. In *Fordham Law Review* 64 (1995): 291.

Fishman, Clifford S. "Consent, Credibility, and the Constitution: Evidence Relating to a Sex Offense Complainant's Past Sexual Behavior." *Catholic University Law Review* 44 (1995): 709.

Forell, Caroline, and Donna Matthews. *A Law of Her Own: The Reasonable Woman as a Measure of Man.* New York: New York University Press, 2000.

Franke, Katherine. "What's Wrong with Sexual Harassment?" *Stanford Law Review* 49 (1997): 691.

Hadfield, Gillian. "Rational Women: A Test for Sex Based Harassment." *California Law Review* 3 (1995): 1151.

MacKinnon, Catharine A. *Sexual Harassment of Working Women: A Case of Sex Discrimination.* New Haven: Yale University Press, 1979.

Pollitt, Katha. "Not Just Bad Sex." *The New Yorker,* October 4, 1993.

Quinn, Sally. "Baggage Check: How Far Should We Go?" *Washington Post,* February 28, 1999.

Reeves Sanday, Peggy. *A Woman Scorned: Acquaintance Rape on Trial.* New York: Doubleday, 1996.

Roiphe, Katie. *The Morning After: Sex, Fear, and Feminism on Campus.* Boston: Little, Brown, 1993.

Schultz, Vicki. "Reconceptualizing Sexual Harassment." *Yale Law Journal* 107 (1998): 1683.

Wolf, Naomi. *Promiscuities: The Secret Struggle for Womanhood.* New York: Random House, 1997.

CHAPTER NINE: POLITICAL POWER

Bellafante, Ginia. "It's All About Me." *Time,* June 29, 1998.

Block, Melissa. "How Women in Suburban Westchester County, New York, Feel About Hillary Clinton's Candidacy for the Senate Seat." National Public Radio's "Morning Edition," March 31, 2000.

Bowman, Karlyn, and Tom Smith. "When Rudy Meets Hillary." *Public Perspective,* August 1999.

Deloitte & Touche. "Women in Elected Office," 2000.

Dolan, Kathleen. "Gender Differences in Support for Women Candidates: Is There a Glass Ceiling in American Politics?" *Women in Politics,* 1997.

———. "Voting for Women in the 'Year of the Woman.'" *American Journal of Political Science* 42 (January 1998).

Dowd, Maureen. "Carville's Cueballers Chalk Up for Giuliani's 'Thugs'." *Denver Post,* December 2, 1999.

EMILY's List. "Campaigning in a Different Voice," Spring 1989.

Green, John C., et al. "Women Big Donors Mobilized in Congressional Elections." Report in "A Study of Individual Contributors to House and Senate Campaigns," June 8 1999.

Heller, Zoe. "Comment: Hillary's Problem Is That Her Drawers Are Messy." *The Daily Telegraph* (London), February 19, 2000.

Kaminer, Wendy. "Feminism's Third Wave: What Do Young Women Want?" *New York Times Book Review,* June 4, 1995.

Interview with feminist Camille Paglia. Fox News Network's "The Edge with Paula Zahn," April 18, 2000.

Klein, Ethel. *Gender Politics: From Consciousness to Mass Politics.* Cambridge, MA: Harvard University Press, 1984.

Mandel, Ruth. "The Political Woman." In *American Women in the Nineties: Today's Critical Issues,* edited by Sherri Matteo. Boston: Northeastern University Press, 1993.

Moore, Martha. "Hillary Clinton Isn't Clicking with Women in NY." *USA Today,* February 10, 2000.

Morin, Richard, and Claudia Deane. "Gender Gap Assumptions Are Giving Rise to Myths." *Washington Post,* April 30, 2000.

Newman, Jody. "Do Women Vote for Women?" *Public Perspective,* February–March 1996.

Roberts, Roxanne. "The Double Life of Hillary Clinton." *Washington Post,* February 8, 2000.

Smith, Tom, and Lance A. Selfa. "When Do Women Vote for Women?" *Public Perspective,* September–October 1992.

CHAPTER TEN: CHANGING OURSELVES

Calvo, Dana. "Female Anchors on Local TV Paid 28 Percent Less." *Los Angeles Times,* June 1, 2000.

Carlson, Margaret. "Does He or Doesn't He?" *Time,* April 27, 1998.

Diamond, Jared. *Why Is Sex Fun? The Evolution of Human Sexuality.* New York: HarperCollins, 1997.

Fallows, Deborah. *A Mother's Work.* Boston: Houghton Mifflin, 1985.

Fox-Genovese, Elizabeth. *Feminism Without Illusions: A Critique of Individualism.* Chapel Hill: University of North Carolina Press, 1991.

Friedan, Betty. *The Feminine Mystique.* New York: Norton, 1963.

Heilbrun, Carolyn. *The Education of a Woman: The Life of Gloria Steinem.* New York: Dial, 1995.

Ireland, Patricia. *What Women Want.* New York: Dutton, 1996.

Kaminer, Wendy. *A Fearful Freedom: Women's Flight from Equality.* Reading, MA: Addison-Wesley, 1990.

Lewis, Diane E. "Homeward Bound: Many Are Trading in Long Hours, Little Satisfaction for Family Time, Peace of Mind." *Boston Globe,* March 29, 1998.

O'Reilly, Jane. "The Housewife's Moment of Truth." *Ms. Magazine,* Spring 1972.

Peters, Joan. *When Mothers Work: Loving Our Children Without Sacrificing Our Selves.* Reading, MA: Addison-Wesley, 1997.

Sellers, Patricia, and Julie Creswell. "The 50 Most Powerful Women in American Business." *Fortune,* October 12, 1998.

Shellenberger, Sue. "Women's Resignation from Top Pepsi Post Rekindles Debate." *Wall Street Journal,* October 8, 1997.

Sigel, Roberta. *Ambition and Accommodation: How Women View Gender Relations.* Chicago: University of Chicago Press, 1996.

Steinem, Gloria. *Revolution from Within: A Book of Self-Esteem.* Boston: Little, Brown, 1992.

Wald, Patricia M. "Glass Ceilings and Open Doors: A Reaction." *Fordham Law Review* 65 (1996): 603.

About the Author

The first woman president of the *Harvard Law Review* and the first woman to run a presidential campaign, Susan Estrich was a professor at Harvard Law School for ten years, and is currently the Robert Kingsley Professor of Law and Political Science at the University of Southern California. She is a nationally syndicated columnist, a contributor to *USA Today,* and a legal and political analyst for *Fox News.* The author of five books, including *Real Rape* and *Getting Away with Murder: How Politics Is Destroying the Criminal Justice System,* Estrich lives in Los Angeles.